YOUTH IN FAMILY
MINISTRY
A HANDBOOK

LUKE DOCKERY

WHAT PEOPLE ARE SAYING ABOUT THIS BOOK…

"Luke Dockery has done the church a great service by writing this concise manual. His approach to developing life-long faith in young people is steeped in Scripture, informed by the latest research, and road tested with real-life experience. Luke clears away the clutter and takes a fresh look at how we can instill lasting faith in our kids. I hope it will be widely read and applied!"

–Joseph Horton, Preaching Minister & Former Youth Minister,
Winchester Church of Christ, Winchester, Tennessee

"If you are serious about helping young people to take ownership of their faith and to grow up as active parts of your local congregation, then you need to read this book. Luke Dockery does not pretend to give a one-size-fits-all method. Instead, he provides a very candid overview of the best research on what facilitates a strong faith commitment in young people and he shares what his own congregation has been doing to take both Scripture and research seriously in crafting an approach for making disciples of the next generation. Luke's candidness and creativity will inspire you, and I am grateful that he has made such a helpful contribution to this deeply important conversation."

–Dr. Mark Adams, Preaching Minister,
Kings Crossing Church of Christ, Corpus Christi, Texas

"In an effective way, Luke takes a crucial issue facing the church and lays out a path forward. Having led a youth ministry for many years and now leading a college ministry, I have seen the often unhealthy effects of parents outsourcing the discipling of their children. Luke, by way of foundational, biblical truth and proven practice, points the church (and families) back to God's original intent of parents discipling their children, and offers practical steps on how the church can aid in that mission. This book is a must-read for any church leader!"

–Jake Greer, Campus Minister, CCSC;
Director of CHRISTeens Youth Conference, Russellville, Arkansas

This book is dedicated to my wife Caroline, my best friend and travel companion on the journey of life. Without your support and encouragement, I would have given up on youth ministry long ago.

Youth In Family Ministry

table of contents

Forward   9
A Note On Youth In Family Ministry

Introduction   11
Better Youth Ministry

A Vanishing Faith   17
The Current Crisis In Youth Ministry

Twin Pillars   37
The Philosophy Of Youth In Family Ministry

Getting To Work   55
Building Youth In Family Ministry In Your Church

Conclusion   77
Jesus Loves the Little Children

Appendix A   81
Youth In Family Ministry In Scripture

Appendix B   93
Resources and Bibliography

Image Credits   103

Forward

a note on youth in family ministry

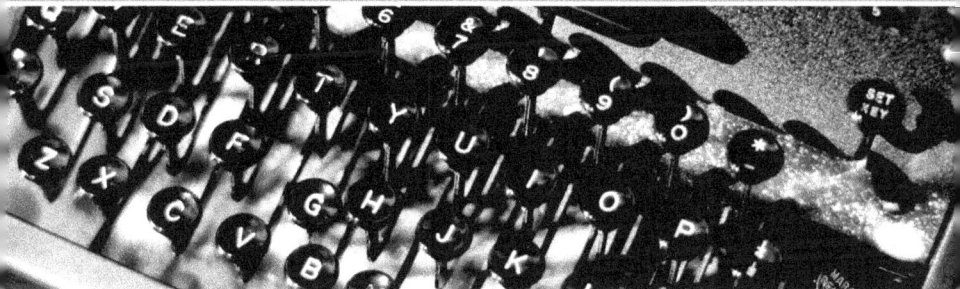

Like many people, I became familiar with youth ministry as a parent. Having three children of my own who were all close in age and very active in youth activities was a challenging, but rewarding, undertaking.

I became acquainted with Luke Dockery in the summer of 2002, when he first came to us at the Farmington Church of Christ as a summer youth ministry intern. I did not really know Luke at all, although I had known his family for quite some time. Thankfully, he was able to come back the following summer, which led to a part-time, and then ultimately, full-time position at our congregation. Since then, I have worked closely with Luke on a number of youth and church-related projects. I respect and value his thoughtful input, and over the years I have come to love and respect him for the true and deep concern he has for the spiritual health of young people. Luke has truly made himself a student of youth ministry.

If you're a parent, I do not have to tell you that working with youth in their formative years is no easy task. Luke takes the work of youth ministry seriously, no matter how daunting the challenge may seem. In *Youth In Family Ministry: A Handbook,* Luke addresses the problems associated with most youth groups in today's churches, namely, age segregation and the absence of mature adult leadership and influence in the lives of our young people. The handbook stresses the importance of both the physical and faith families, giving biblical examples of what God intended regarding the rearing of our children. This is not a new way of thinking, but rather an old philosophy resurrected.

Although intergenerational ministry is vitally important, a proper balance of youth group activities is necessary for interaction and relationship building among the group itself. This balance of activities creates the healthy environment that a congregation needs in order to develop interactions between those in the youth group and the aged, seasoned Christians that can help and encourage them in their spiritual walk.

As mentioned earlier, raising children is one of the most challenging tasks that has been given to us while on this earth. Thank God for men like Luke, who devote their lives to not only helping our kids become better kids, but also helping parents become better parents. *Youth In Family Ministry: A Handbook* is a well-thought-out, bible-based resource. Read and put into practice the insightful thoughts this handbook offers and may God bless you as you engage in Youth in Family Ministry!

Marion Bailey
Shepherd over Youth Ministry
Farmington Church of Christ

Introduction
better youth ministry

The Purpose of this Book

For over a decade now, I have had the honor of serving as the Associate Minister of the Farmington Church of Christ. In that role, I do a lot of different things, but my primary responsibility is to oversee the youth ministry of the Farmington church, which, as you will see, we call *Youth In Family Ministry*.

After working as a youth minister for several years, I began to notice a few things about the way youth ministry is frequently practiced that bothered me:

- First, I was frustrated by how common it seemed to be for a lot of parents to outsource the task of teaching their children about Jesus and the Bible to a youth minister.

- Second, I was disturbed by studies which showed that an alarming number of teenagers leave their faith behind after high school.

- Finally, I didn't like how often youth ministry seemed to be, well, kind of shallow. I enjoy playing games and eating pizza as much as the next guy, but it seems to me that youth ministry should be about a lot more than providing childcare and wholesome entertainment.

With this in mind, I began to think about the things we did in our youth ministry at Farmington. Specifically, I wondered if there wasn't a better, more biblical way to go about the process of teaching our young people what it means to be disciples of Jesus Christ in a way that would stick with them throughout their lives. I began to read a lot of books, study Scripture, talk to other youth ministers, and I even wrote a couple of research papers on the topic. Eventually, after a lot of twists and turns, that process led to the book you are holding in your hands (or reading on your screen).

This book specifically addresses the first two problems mentioned above, and based on the teachings of Scripture, the research of youth ministry experts, and my own experiences, attempts to provide a model of youth ministry that connects young people to the congregation as a whole and seeks to grow within them a faith that will last for life. I do not claim that it is a finished or perfect product; rather, it is a blueprint of how I think congregational youth ministry should operate, and it is the model we are attempting to follow at our church.[1]

As we discover flaws (and we undoubtedly will), we will seek to correct them, always with the goal in mind of helping our young people develop a mature and lasting faith in Jesus Christ.

This handbook is wide in scope and is written with several different audiences in mind:

- It is written for **parents and grandparents** who are trying to raise

---

[1] Addressing the third problem—the shallowness that is a common characteristic of youth ministry—lies beyond the scope of this book. However, specifically to confront this issue, I helped to establish Deeper Youth Ministry, an organization that seeks to help young people develop a deeper, more mature faith in Christ. See www.deeperyouthministry.com for more information.

their children and grandchildren in the Lord and are looking for support from the church as they seek to fulfill this sacred duty. You have been called to an important task, but thankfully you do not have to do it alone!

- It is written for **members of local churches** who want to know what they can do as parts of the Body of Christ to train up children in the Lord. The young people at your church need you, and as a member of Christ's Body, you have the responsibility to help them develop their faith.

- It is especially written for **youth ministers and church leaders** who are looking for ways to improve their youth ministry practices. If you spend your time working with students and seeking to lead them to a life of following Jesus, I appreciate your devotion to young people and to the cause of Christ. As you will see in the following pages, I think the way youth ministry has traditionally been practiced is flawed and needs to be changed. Having said that, I still think that when youth ministry is done properly, it is a vital part of helping young people to become disciples of Jesus. So let me encourage you to continue your work in youth ministry, and to do it well!

Stewardship and Youth Ministry

Often when we think about the word **stewardship** we immediately think of money and how we spend it, but stewardship is about a lot more than that. Stewardship just means being responsible for and taking care of something with which you have been entrusted, and from that perspective, I think more discussions about youth ministry need to take place with the idea of stewardship in mind.

Perhaps more than any other idea in this book, I want you to come away with this: **God has entrusted us—both in our physical families and in our church family—with *His* children. We tend to think of them as *ours*, but truly, ultimately, they are *His*.** "Our" children belong to God. Put another way, children are God's gift to us (Psalm 127.3), and what we do with our children is our gift to God. John Wesley once said:

[Children are] immortal spirits whom God hath, for a time, entrusted to your care, that you may train them up in all holiness, and fit them for the enjoyment of God in eternity. This is a glorious and important trust; seeing one soul is of more value than all the world beside. Every child, therefore, you are to watch over with the utmost care, that, when you are called to give an account of each to the Father of spirits, you may give your accounts with joy and not with grief. [2]

God expects us to take care of His kids, and a primary part of that task is that we are responsible for their spiritual growth. We are to bring them up in the Lord, and I want you to know that as a father and as a youth minister, I am determined to be a good steward of the most precious things which God has given us—our children.

A Closing Thought

As you read this book, my hope is that you will come to a better understanding of what Youth In Family Ministry is all about, and will also see how this model is informed by the teachings of Scripture. Ultimately, I think youth ministry should be about encouraging young people to become lifelong disciples of Jesus, and this handbook explains how I think that very important task should be accomplished.

I wanted this handbook to be as comprehensive as possible, but of course, there is no way to anticipate every single question or address every possible

---

[2] As cited in Timothy Paul Jones, *Family Ministry Field Guide: How Your Church Can Equip Parents to Make Disciples* (Indianapolis: Wesleyan Publishing House, 2011): 79.

concern. If, as you read, a question comes to mind, feel free to get in touch with me (my contact information is available at the end of the book). I care deeply about young people and helping them come to a mature and lasting faith in Jesus Christ, and if you are involved in that process as a parent, grandparent, minister, elder, deacon, or in any other way, I am happy to assist you however I can.

I have several people to thank for their help with this project:

- Thanks to Marion Bailey, the shepherd who oversees the youth ministry at the congregation where I work, for his support and encouragement over the years, and for writing the Forward of this book.

- I greatly appreciate my dear friends Justin Bland, Kevin Burr, Whit Jordan, Jared Pack, and Mike Raine, who each read versions of this manuscript and offered invaluable suggestions. This book would be a lesser product without their input.

- I am deeply indebted to my parents, who were certainly the "primary spiritual influencers" in my life growing up, and to the many adult Christians from my faith family at the Baldwin Church of Christ who invested in my life and showed me that I was important to them.

- Thank you to my wife Caroline, who has been by my side every step of the way, and to whom this book is dedicated.

- And of course, thanks to God, who patiently persuaded a young man who had no desire to go into ministry that He had other plans for him.

To Him be all the glory as we do our utmost to pass our faith on to His children!

Luke Dockery
August 2018

A Vanishing Faith

Disappearing Christians

It is necessary that we start with the bad news: a large percentage of teenagers who have committed their lives to Christ and are active in church life walk away from that commitment after graduating from high school and their youth groups.

Although a lot of research has been done on this specific topic, it is difficult to get an exact percentage of just how many teens leave the church after high school, as different studies suggest a range of statistics. These different numbers can be explained by several factors:

- These studies want to determine the faithfulness of teens after high school, but how do you define *faithful*? Different definitions of faithfulness across studies (e.g., attending church two times per *week* versus attending church two times per *month*) will obviously yield different results.

- Some studies look at a particular denomination or religious group, while others are broader in scope.

17

- Surveys are conducted at different times, and information like this, especially in a country like the United States that is becoming increasingly secularized, can change rapidly.

- Different surveys cover different age ranges.

All of these factors help to explain why you can find a variety of statistics on this, but a good general estimate is that between 40-50% of teenagers leave their faith behind after high school.[3]

Dr. Flavil Yeakley, a statistician from Harding University, did a study focusing particularly on Churches of Christ and found that over 40% of students leave the church after growing up and leaving home, with 21% abandoning their faith altogether, and another 21% retaining their faith, but leaving Churches of Christ to join denominational groups.[4]

The fact that one-fifth of our young people are joining denominational churches after high school is important, and the implications of that statistic are worth discussing, but ultimately, those issues are beyond the scope of this book. Needless to say, having these young people leave our fellowship is certainly not ideal.

With all of that in mind, I think 40-50% of teens leaving the church is a fairly conservative estimate to work with, and before we proceed further, there are a few points I want to make here:

- First, this is a serious problem, but it is one which is often overstated.

---

[3] Kara E. Powell and Chap Clark, *Sticky Faith: Everyday Ideas to Build Lasting Faith in Your Kids* (Grand Rapids: Zondervan, 2011): 15. Other sources suggest different percentages. Kendra Creasy Dean, "Proclaiming Salvation: Youth Ministry for the Twenty-First Century Church," *Theology Today* 56, no. 4 (January 2000): 525, states that "more than half of those confirmed as adolescents leave the church by age seventeen."

[4] Flavil R. Yeakley, Jr., *Why They Left: Listening to Those Who Have Left Churches of Christ* (Nashville: Gospel Advocate, 2012): 39.

Some sources suggest that we are losing 80-90% of our young people, and as far as I can tell that figure is simply inaccurate. I have found no reliable research that suggests a number anywhere close to that. The reality (40-50%) is bad enough; there is no need to exaggerate it.[5]

• Second, "only 20 percent of college students who leave the faith planned to do so during high school. The remaining 80 percent intended to stick with their faith but didn't."[6] We all know that there are some kids who go to church because they are forced to by their parents and are not particularly committed. But people like this only account for a small percentage of those who are leaving. Four-fifths of those students who leave their faith behind during college *had no intention of doing so.* That's significant.

• Third, it is important for us to realize and acknowledge that college and young adulthood is a time when people naturally want to try a lot of new things and figure out for themselves who they are and what they want to do in life. It is during this time that a lot of young people stray from the church. However, this period of searching and experimentation is, generally speaking, a temporary process, and many teens who leave the church after high school actually *return* in their late 20s when their lives have become more settled. Somewhere between 30-60% of youth group

---

5 Wesley Black, "Youth Ministry That Lasts: The Faith Journey of Young Adults," *Journal of Youth Ministry* 4, no. 2 (Spring 2006): 19, cites a Southern Baptist Convention study which found that "88 percent of the children raised in evangelical homes leave church at the age of 18, never to return." This statistic has been repeated with great frequency, but upon further examination, seems to be based on the personal estimates of two youth ministry practitioners rather than actual research. See Jones, 46-47. Of course, that doesn't mean that there are not *individual churches or congregations* that are losing a much higher percentage of their young people than 40-50%.

6 Powell and Clark, 16.

A Vanishing
FAITH
teens after high school

45% OF CHRISTIAN TEENS WALK AWAY FROM THEIR FAITH AFTER HIGH SCHOOL

Only 20% planned to leave their faith behind...

...which means 80% did not.

In Churches of Christ:

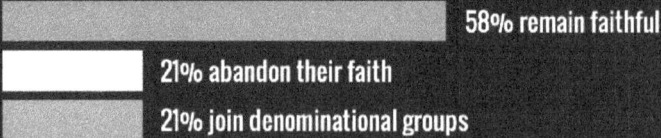

58% remain faithful

21% abandon their faith

21% join denominational groups

SOURCES: Kara E. Powell and Chap Clark, Sticky Faith: Everyday Ideas to Build Lasting Faith in Your Kids (Grand Rapids: Zondervan, 2011); Flavil R. Yeakley, Jr., Why They Left: Listening to Those Who Have Left Churches of Christ (Nashville: Gospel Advocate, 2012).

DYM

graduates who abandon their faith return *to* it in their late 20s.[7] Now, that's good news, but it still means that 40-70% of those who leave do *not* return. And for those who do return, their time away from the church has been significant: many have already made choices in life regarding who they are going to marry, what career they are going to pursue, and what their worldview and priorities will be, and they made those decisions while they were away from the church at a time when faith was not playing a significant role in their decision-making. Furthermore, the time away from the church represents nearly a decade of lost opportunity for service and spiritual growth.[8]

So, we don't want to overstate the case by saying that more young people are leaving than actually are or by saying that they'll never come back, but at the same time, the reality is bad enough: 40-50% are leaving, and many of them do not come back.

And I guess the obvious question here is *Why?* We know that this alarming trend is occurring, but *why* is it occurring?

This is a complicated issue, and there are several different factors involved in why so many Christian teens leave the church after high school:

- **More personal responsibility:** whether teens go to college after high school or simply move out and begin working, they are less under the influence of their parents and more responsible for making their own decisions. Will they choose to wake up on Sunday morning in time to

---

[7] Ibid.

[8] This stage of life can be an excellent one for service to the church, as work and family responsibilities are generally not as demanding at this time. There are numerous faithful Christians in their 20s in our church family at Farmington who are ministry leaders or who have been active in mission work, specifically *because* this stage of life affords them the time to serve in these capacities.

go to church? Will they plan Saturday night activities that enable them to get to bed at an hour where they *can* get up and go to church on Sunday?

- **Greater peer influence:** with the lessened influence of parents, there is an increase in peer influence. What if none of their friends are Christians?

- **A Distorted view of the Gospel:** Too often, our kids reduce the Christian faith to a checklist of do's and don'ts aimed at good behavior and the limiting of sin.[9] But it is both spiritually exhausting and practically impossible to check off all the right behavioral boxes, and when many students realize this, rather than seeking a deeper, more genuine faith, they simply give up.

- **Limited free time:** college brings a new level of busyness: classes, labs, study groups, and social activities. Teens who don't go to college but begin working full-time instead are also very busy. With such full schedules, it is easy for church involvement and spiritual disciplines like Bible reading and prayer to get squeezed out.

- **The "Philosophy 101 Effect":** this refers to the stereotypical state school scenario where in a class on philosophy or the history of religion, students are exposed to the idea that Jesus was just a wise teacher, not God's Son, and the Bible is just a book of religious traditions, not God's Word. Similarly, in science courses students are taught that the universe has naturalistic origins that exclude the idea of a Creator. If Christian students were not taught very well or very deeply to begin with and they are not equipped to respond to these claims, this can be incredibly

---

[9] Kara E. Powell, *The Sticky Faith Guide For Your Family* (Grand Rapids, MI: Zondervan, 2014): 43-44. This idea, the "Gospel of Sin Management," comes from Dallas Willard's *The Divine Conspiracy.*

damaging to their faith.[10]

So there are a lot of different reasons for this trend, and we haven't even mentioned the biggest reason, or, the problem which ministry experts and researchers have cited and focused on the most. That problem is age segregation, or, the way that "churches have systematically isolated young people from the very relationships that are most likely to lead them to maturity."[11] This is part of a larger issue that exists in our society, where children, and especially teens, have less frequent contact with adults (including their parents) than ever before.

Age Segregation in our Society

In preindustrial Europe and extending into the American colonies, young people spent a lot of time around adults, especially around their families. In rural settings, the vast majority of young people grew up to work in agriculture as their parents before them and learned how to farm by working alongside their parents throughout their young lives. Life in urban settings was somewhat different, but still involved significant close interaction between young people and adults, as young people were regularly taken on as apprentices and worked closely with an adult

[10] Rob Bell, *Velvet Elvis: Repainting the Christian Faith* (Grand Rapids, MI: Zondervan, 2005): 81, discusses this specific scenario, and the trouble that comes from having a faith that is not "big enough" to handle the knew information that a student is exposed to in college.

[11] Mark DeVries, *Family-Based Youth Ministry,* Rev. ed. (Downers Grove, IL: InterVarsity Press, 2004): 36.

A family works together on a Delaware farm in 1910.

craftsman in order to learn a trade.[12]

Even well into the 20th century, kids might go to school, but then would come home and work side by side on the farm with their parents. They would work alongside their parents on the weekends as well . That's not what happens anymore. A lot of kids cannot even explain what their parents do for a living, and they certainly don't do it alongside them!

Furthermore, in previous eras young people grew up in constant contact with grandparents and other members of the extended family—aunts, uncles, and cousins—in a way that is rare today. Only a few generations ago, it was common for people to live their entire lives within a radius of a few hundred miles, but through advances in transportation, people are more mobile now than ever before. As a result, it is common for people to grow up and move

---

[12] Theresa O'Keefe, "Growing Up Alone: The New Normal of Isolation in Adolescence," *The Journal of Youth Ministry* 13, no. 1 (September 2014): 74-78. O'Keefe examines the lives of young people in Medieval England in some detail, and contrasts that with 21st century America: "This was a world where a young person was known well by by the adults around them. The world of adolescents and adults was in large part the same social world. These factors stand in dramatic contrast to the twenty-first century world, where adolescents and adults live largely segregated lives—spending their days in separate pursuits."

away from their homes in search of work, and extended families are spread apart all across the country, or sometimes, world.[13]

Gradually, after we slowly transitioned to a more urban, more mobile, service-oriented society and economy, it became increasingly common for both parents to work. While it was once true that kids would come home after school and stay with their mothers until their fathers got home from their jobs, today, many children grow up in one-parent homes or in two-parent homes where both parents work. As a result, many kids come home to an empty house, or stay longer at school in after-school programs or at sports practices.[14]

Young people are simply not around adults as much as they used to be. One particularly disturbing study illustrates the extreme unavailability of adults in teenagers' lives, revealing that teens spend less than seven percent of their waking hours with direct contact with adults.[15] Certainly teenagers spend time *around* adults, as a significant portion of their time is spent at school, in structured classrooms with adult teachers. However, in these situations teens

---

[13] Faith Kirkham Hawkins, "Ministry With Youth...Without Youth Ministry," *Insights* 123, no. 2 (Spring 2008): 29; Harold J. Hinrichs, "Intergenerational Living and Worship: The Caring Community," *Journal of Religion and Aging* 3, nos. 1-2 (September 1986): 185.

[14] This is not to suggest that it is *wrong* for both parents to work; it is simply an acknowledgement that times have changed, and these changes significantly affect the interactions between parents and children.

[15] Mihaly Csiksgentmihalyi and Carson Reed, *Being Adolescent: Conflict and Growth in the Teenage Years* (New York: Basic Books, 1984), 70-75. These statistics are now dated, but considering that the societal trends of isolation discussed above have only *increased* since this research was completed, the pervasiveness of age isolation is clear.

are part of a large group, competing with other students for the teacher's attention.[16]

Regardless of the popular conception of teenagers locking themselves in their rooms and blaring their music to get away from their parents, age segregation is *not* what they *desire*. "Young adolescents do not want to be left to their own devices. In national surveys and focus groups, America's youth have given voice to a serious longing. They want more regular contact with adults who care about and respect them."[17]

Age segregation is not *good* for young people either, since they learn how to *be* adults by *being around* adults: "in all societies since the beginning of time, adolescents have learned to become adults by observing, imitating and interacting with grown-ups around them....it is therefore startling how little time [modern] teenagers spend in the company of adults."[18]

Furthermore, much of the direct, one-on-one time which youth *do* have with adults occurs in "...role-specific ways with adults who are paid to spend time with them."[19] This includes teachers, coaches, and youth ministers. Good things can certainly come from those associations, but the frequency with which those roles change (e.g., students get new teachers every year) makes it

---

[16] Csiksgentmihalyi and Reed, 73-74, "Almost never did these students report talking personally to a teacher...their only contact with them was as authority figures." DeVries, 91, astutely and sadly observes, "It has become a novelty for a teenager and an adult to have more than a passing conversation". Powell, *The Sticky Faith Guide For Your Family,* 97: "only 45 percent of middle and high school students have three or more caring adults (outside of their parents) they can turn to for advice and support).

[17] *A Matter of Time: Risk and Opportunity in the Nonschool Hours. Report of the Task Force on Youth Development and Community Programs,* (Washington, DC: Carnegie Council on Adolescent Development, 1992): 11.

[18] Csiksgentmihalyi and Reed, 73.

[19] Don C. Richter, Doug Magnuson, and Michael Baizerman, "Reconceiving Youth Ministry," *Religious Education* 93, no. 3 (Summer 1998): 349.

CHAP CLARK: AGE SEGREGATION HURTS YOUNG PEOPLE

In 2001, well-known youth ministry expert and researcher Chap Clark embarked on a multi-year study in order to better understand what it is like to be an adolescent in today's society. In 2004, he published his research findings in Hurt: Inside The World Of Today's Teenagers. The book became a classic in youth ministry studies, and was significantly revised and expanded in 2011 as Hurt 2.0.

Clark emphasizes how difficult life is for young people today due to the fact that systemic isolation from adults leaves them feeling abandoned and forces them to figure out how to grow up largely on their own. Clark's analysis is biting, but is something that adults need to hear:

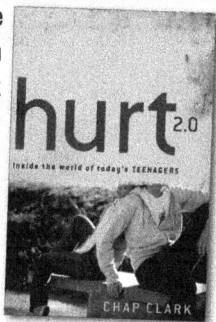

[From a student] "I can't ever find someone to talk to who knows how I am feeling. My parents always say that they know how I feel and that they have been there, but times have changed....I wish I could find someone to talk to who knows me and understands me" (26).

"The fact is that adolescents need adults to become adults, and when adults are not present and involved in their lives, they are forced to figure out how to survive life on their own" (26-27).

"The loss of meaningful relationships with adults has been the most devastating to developing adolescents" (35).

"Adolescents notice when they do not get to spend enough time with parents and other adults. In facilitating a parent/youth event for a community group in Seattle last fall, I asked students to compile a list of what they wanted adults to know about them. One of the most telling statements they recorded was how they perceived time with significant adults: 'We spend no time with adults from junior high on—maybe fifteen minutes every other day is the best we ever get.' It is as though adults don't understand that time spent with significant adults, especially parents, provides the most important environment for healthy adolescent development" (38).

"In sum, systemic abandonment by institutions and adults who are in positions originally designed to care for adolescents has created a culture of isolation" (40).

SOURCE: Chap Clark, Hurt 2.0: Inside the World of Today's Teenagers (Grand Rapids: Baker Academic, 2011).

difficult to develop deep and lasting relationships.[20] Also, when young people only get to be around adults when they are operating in a specific role, they are deprived of the opportunity to see the "multi-faceted nature of adult lives" and learn first-hand how mature adults deal with the daily issues of life.[21] In other words, while relationships with teachers, coaches, and youth ministers can be valuable, they cannot take the place of kids having multiple relationships with mature adults from whom they can naturally learn and upon whom they can lean on as they grow and mature in life.

Age Segregation in the Church

Unfortunately, the widespread problem of age segregation is not limited to our society, as it has also become very common within the church. This was not always the case, though.

Churches in the New Testament occurred in the household setting, which provided a natural opportunity for children to learn and worship alongside adults.[22] Even as the setting for gatherings of the church changed from private homes to church buildings and cathedrals, this combination of young people with adults remained the common practice for hundreds of years.[23]

The Great Reformation of the 16th century brought about many needed changes to church practices of the time, including an emphasis on the

---

[20] O'Keefe, 80.

[21] Ibid., 83.

[22] Allan G. Harkness, "Intergenerational Christian Education: An Imperative for Effective Education in Local Churches, Part 1," *Journal of Christian Education* 41, no. 2 (July 1998): 7.

[23] O'Keefe, 71-72: "In the medieval church there was no concept of religious programming for youth, as understood today. Rather children and youth were simply part of the wider congregation, participating in worship and prayer as they were able."

importance of reading and teaching the Bible as the dominant source of church doctrine and practice. An unfortunate by-product of this emphasis on teaching was neglect of other aspects of church life in which children and young people were more easily included. That, combined with Renaissance conceptualizations of children as "little adults" led to the increased marginalization and isolation of children and young people in congregational life.[24]

As these understandings of children changed over time, churches began to focus more on children as persons in their own right, and borrowing the schooling model from public education, began to separate children by age in order to teach them about faith. The Sunday school movement began in the 19th century on these foundations, as did parachurch ministries like the Young Men's Christian Association (YMCA), and continue to the present day.[25]

Churches of Christ are spiritual heirs of the Stone-Campbell Restoration Movement of the early-19th century, which called people to leave man-made religious denominations and simply be a part of the church described in the pages of the New Testament. Although the Restoration Movement was distinctive in several areas, including its emphasis on baptism for the remission of sins and the worship and organization of the church, it shared in the Reformation ideal of the importance of biblical education, and largely followed denominational practices with regard to educating children. In other words, Churches of Christ, while consciously and intentionally distinctive from denominational groups in many ways, have not been particularly

---

[24] Harkness, 7.

[25] Ibid, 7; Allan G. Harkness, "Intergenerational Corporate Worship as a Significant Educational Activity," *Christian Education Journal* 7, no. 1 (2003): 13; Darwin Glassford and Lynn Barger-Elliot, "Toward Intergenerational Ministry in a Post-Christian Era," *Christian Education Journal* 8, no. 2 (September 2011): 367.

distinctive when it comes to ministry with young people.[26] As denominational groups employed a variety of age-segregated means to work with young people in a targeted way—beginning Sunday school programs, developing Vacation Bible School programs in the summer, running bus ministries to bring kids into church whose parents were not believers, and ultimately hiring youth ministers to work directly with young people— Churches of Christ basically followed suit.

These noble efforts derived from the recognition of the distinctive spiritual needs of young people and an attempt to address those needs. Over time, however, the cumulative effect of these efforts led to a church culture where young people are systematically isolated from adults just as they are in society at large.[27]

In churches, age segregation is played out in a number of ways. Consider some of the following common youth ministry practices which result in separating young people from the rest of the congregation:

- Early on, children are divided into classes based on age. They will spend their entire lives as children and teenagers in these age groups, learning alongside peers and being taught by an assortment of adults over time.

- During worship, it is thought that kids cannot behave or might not understand what is going on, so they are separated from their parents and other adults in order to have children's church in another location.

- As kids grow older, it is important for them to have more activities to be involved in, so a youth minister is paid to interact with and take care of

[26] By saying "Churches of Christ" with a capital "C", I am not attempting to denominate the church; I am simply reflecting the terminology used in sociological and historical studies.

[27] Hinrichs, 183, describing common practice in the modern church, says, "The norm is fragmentation in congregational life."

young people so parents and other adults do not have to.

- The youth group might actually meet for class in their own separate building which is isolated from everyone else.

- Instead of meeting at the building with "old people" on Sunday nights, the youth group will gather in a special small group, meeting in each other's homes to have a devotional, sing songs, and then have a meal.

- Many Sundays the youth group is not present at all, because it is a priority for them to be gone to as many trips and youth rallies as possible on weekends. Perhaps the thought is that it is hard to keep teens excited about just going to "regular" church.

- On Wednesday nights, there will be a special youth group class in the youth building. At no point will they meet with the rest of the congregation during the evening, but rather remain in their building to have more time with one another.

- Also, the youth group will frequently participate in special youth worship services where all the teens from the area meet together.

To be clear, I am not suggesting that these activities are necessarily wrong, and in fact, we do some of these things in the youth ministry that I lead. For example, we generally think it is a good idea to divide Bible classes by age level so children can be taught appropriately. We also have a paid youth minister (it's me!), and I am certainly not campaigning that they fire me. So please do not get onto the youth minister or elders at your church because some book you read said they were doing youth ministry all wrong! That is not what I am saying. Most likely the people who are directing the youth ministry at your church are doing what they think is best, what they have been taught, or what they have witnessed other churches do.

But I do want to raise the question: what happens when you take *all* of these practices and combine them together? The net result is that by the time teens have graduated from high school, they may have spent a great deal of time doing "church activities" with a youth group, but have had little, real interaction with the church as a whole, and that is a problem.[28]

This isolation has been creatively described as the "one-eared Mickey Mouse,"[29] where the youth program is almost like a tumor growing off to the side of the rest of the church—only peripherally connected.

In a sense, the youth group becomes something like a parallel congregation;[30] youth group members don't know adult Christians unless it is

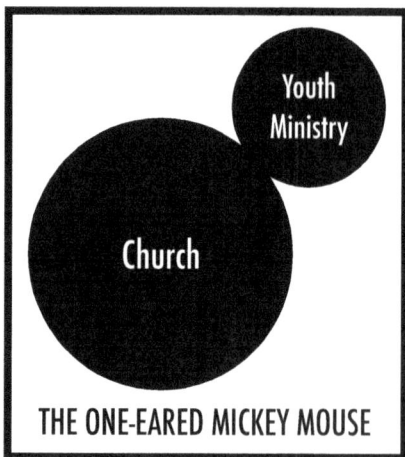

THE ONE-EARED MICKEY MOUSE

a minister, a relative, or the parent of a friend. When you think of it this way, it's no surprise that so many teens leave the church once they graduate from the youth group; they were never really part of the congregation to begin with![31]

Not only is the practice of separating young people from the rest of the congregation harmful to the development of lifelong faith in youth, it is also

---

[28] Holly Catterton Allen and Christine Lawton Ross, *Intergenerational Christian Formation: Bringing the Whole Church Together in Ministry, Community and Worship* (Downers Grove, IL: IVP Academic, 2012): 193, "To many Christians in America, parents and children worshiping together has become an uncommon experience."

[29] DeVries, 42.

[30] Carol Duerksen, *Building Together: Developing Your Blueprint for Congregational Youth Ministry* (Newton, KS: Faith & Life Resources, 2001): 42.

[31] John Roberto, "Our Future Is Intergenerational," *Christian Education Journal* 3rd ser., 9 (Spring 2012): 110, "Teenagers do not leave the church; the church and teens were never introduced!"

> It's no surprise that so many teens LEAVE THE CHURCH once they graduate from the youth group; they were never really PART OF THE CONGREGATION to begin with!

harmful to the congregation. As one author points out, "Just as it would hurt the physical body to detach limbs, it also damages the spiritual body when we disengage with one another."[32] The removal of young people prevents the rest of the community of faith from benefitting from the strengths and abilities of the younger generation.[33]

In most traditional youth ministry programs, age segregation extends even to families, as parents are typically separated from their teens, and the task of spiritual formation is outsourced to a youth minister. This divorce of parents from the work of discipling their children is extremely unfortunate: as we will see, it is not only a departure from the biblical example of how faith should be passed on to young people, but also, research overwhelmingly indicates that parents are the "primary spiritual influencers of their children."[34] This might come as a surprise to many parents, but the reality is that parents do not simply have more spiritual influence on their kids than the *church* does; they

---

[32] Allen and Ross, 114.

[33] Hawkins, 29.

[34] Brenda Snailum, "Implementing Intergenerational Youth Ministry Within Existing Evangelical Church Congregations: What Have We Learned?" *Christian Education Journal,* 3rd ser., 9 (Spring 2012): 173.

have more influence over them than *any* group does.[35] One author's research suggests that churches only have about 40 hours of influence per year with a young person, while the average parent has approximately 3,000 hours per year to spend with their children.[36]

For parents who are reading this, this reality should be both empowering and humbling to you. It should be empowering because it means that you have the ability and opportunity to be a great spiritual and moral influence on your children. At the same time, it should be humbling (and maybe even a little scary) because it means that you must be careful to use your influence with your children in the right way.

To put it another way, since children are so greatly influenced by what their parents do, unless a parent is also involved in the process of spiritual formation in teens, the efforts of a youth minister are unlikely to be effective.

It is hard to out-teach the home.

A Determination To Do Better

The reality is that a lot of young people are leaving the church after high school. What's worse is that some of the very youth ministry practices that have been used to *help* young people are, in fact, *harming* them.

---

[35] Black, 20, "Many facts contribute to the development of religious involvement among youth, but parents easily constitute the strongest influence, whether positive or negative."

[36] Reggie Joiner, *Think Orange: Imagine The Impact When Church And Family Collide* (Colorado Springs: David C. Cook, 2009): 85-88. Of course, that does not mean that parents actually *take advantage* of that significant amount of time, or that all of that time is of the same quality that the church gets. See also Reggie Joiner and Tom Shefchunas, *Lead Small: Five Big Ideas Every Small Group Leader Needs To Know* (Cumming, GA: reThink Group, 2012): 99. Csiksgentmihalyi and Reed, 59, "At home, adolescents spend the largest proportion of their waking hours (and also, their sleeping time) in their bedrooms. This begins to suggest that the home is not only a setting of family interaction but also a context of solitary withdrawal."

YEARLY INFLUENCE ON YOUNG PEOPLE:
PARENTS VS. THE CHURCH

(EACH ● EQUALS FIVE HOURS)

THE CHURCH

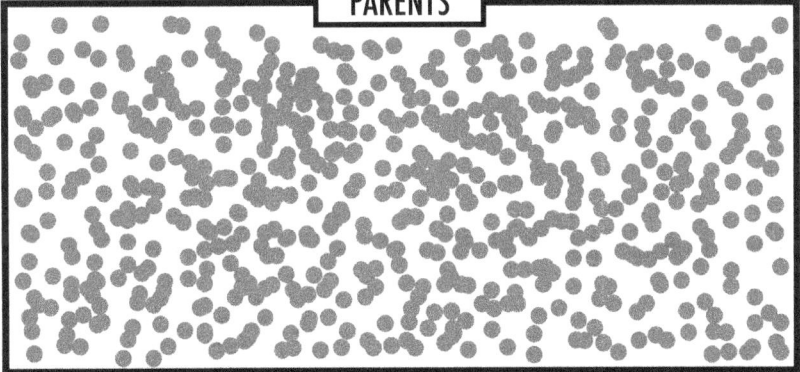

PARENTS

SOURCE: Reggie Joiner, *Think Orange: Imagine The Impact When Church And Family Collide* (Colorado Springs: David C. Cook, 2009): 85-88.

35

That is a sobering reality, but we shouldn't respond to it by throwing up our hands in despair; rather, we should determine to do a better job in ministering to young people. What does the Bible teach us about passing faith on to the next generation? What insight can research studies share with us about developing lasting faith in our kids? It is to these questions that we will fix our attention in the next chapter.

Questions for Reflection

1. Have you observed the problem of teenagers abandoning their faith after high school? Does the 40-50% statistic seem accurate in your congregation?

2. Several reasons were given for why young people might leave their faith behind after high school; what other reasons can you think of?

3. What practices in your congregation reflect the problem of age segregation?

Twin Pillars

the philosophy of youth in family ministry

Seeking a More Biblical Youth Ministry

As we saw in the last chapter, our society is plagued by the problem of age segregation, and the way that youth ministry has traditionally been practiced has done a lot to aggravate that problem. What if there is a better way? What if, instead of systematically *separating* young people from the very people who can show them what mature Christian life looks like, we intentionally *brought them together?* That is what Youth In Family Ministry (and this book) is all about.

In Scripture, over and over again we read about two groups having the primary responsibility of passing faith on to young people: the **physical family** and the **faith family**. When I say "physical family", I am talking about the flesh and blood families in which our young people are raised: mothers, fathers, siblings, grandparents, adoptive parents, and legal guardians. By "faith family", I mean the community of faith in which a young person grows up (whether that is the people of Israel in the Old Testament or the church in the New Testament).

That's why our youth ministry at the Farmington church is called "Youth *In* Family Ministry," because we are trying to work with our young people and help them grow within the context of family. The usual terminology you hear is "Youth *and* Family Ministry," but I am intentionally avoiding that phrasing and going in a different direction. I think that the words we use are important, and that they influence the way we think about things. With that in mind, I do not want to give the impression that "youth ministry" and "family ministry" are two separate things. Instead, I want to focus on ministering to young people *in the context* of family, both the physical family and the church family.

At this point I want to emphasize that when I talk about Youth In Family Ministry as a model for the way we should work with our young people, it is something that I advocate primarily not because I think it is *effective* (although I do), but because I think it is *biblical.* I am not comfortable with just going out and doing things in order to get results if the things we are doing are unbiblical. When it comes to this model of youth ministry, though, I think it absolutely is biblical. Furthermore, it shouldn't surprise us that following what the Bible teaches is effective as well, and indeed, that is what the research shows: a much more effective means of discipling children comes from the physical family and the entire church congregation combining their strengths and efforts to work together to instill long-term faith in young people.[37]

Based on the guidance of Scripture, **physical family** and **faith family** are the twin pillars of our youth ministry. Together, they provide the foundation for the way in which we hope to bring about lasting spiritual formation in our young people. And I want to be very clear here that *both* of these pillars need to be emphasized. The physical family and the faith family are both vital when it comes to helping young people to become spiritually mature Christians. In fact, I think there is a real danger of focusing too much on one pillar and neglecting the other.

---

[37] Joiner, 24-27.

THE TWIN PILLARS OF YOUTH IN FAMILY MINISTRY

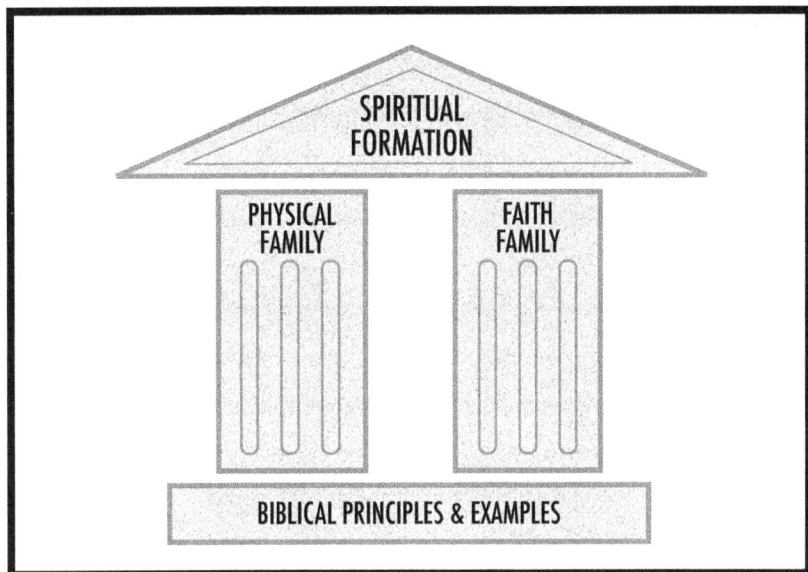

```
                    SPIRITUAL
                    FORMATION

    PHYSICAL              FAITH
    FAMILY                FAMILY




       BIBLICAL PRINCIPLES & EXAMPLES
```

This may not be a popular point, but sometimes, we place too much emphasis on our physical families. We live in a society where broken families are a huge problem, and in a well-meaning effort to deal with this very real problem, I think churches have sometimes over-corrected and almost made physical families an idol. At times, the goal of a having a healthy family and happy, well-adjusted children is made to be the most important pursuit in life. Discipleship takes a back seat. I've actually heard parents before talk about how they were missing *worship* because they needed to have some "family time". This is a problem—clearly, we can overemphasize the physical family!

Other times, though, we are guilty of placing such a great emphasis on activities with our faith families that it becomes a detriment to the physical family. In addition to our regular worship and assembly times, we schedule a range of other activities, and at certain times, there is some "church" event or obligation every night of the week! I believe that Christians have a lot of work to do to carry out God's mission, and that means that the church *should* be busy, but when many of these activities are structured in ways which are not very family-friendly, the end result is that parents' attempts to be involved in the work of the church actually leads them to neglect their physical families! That, too, is a problem.

Both the faith family and the physical family are important. They both need to be emphasized, and both are vital to the spiritual formation of young people. If either of these indispensable pillars is removed, the entire structure of Youth In Family Ministry comes crashing down and the spiritual formation it seeks to develop in our young people is completely undermined.

The Physical Family

We'll begin by looking more closely at the first major pillar of Youth In Family Ministry: the physical family unit.

In youth ministry studies, the emphasis on the importance of the physical family in ministry to young people is referred to as "family ministry." Authors can mean different things when using that term, but the heart of family ministry is organizing the practices of a congregation "so that parents are acknowledged, trained, and held accountable as primary disciple-makers in their children's lives."[38] Related to this, it is important to emphasize that family ministry is not just another *program* to add an existing list of church programs. Instead, it is a *mindset* that informs how those other programs should function —with the strengthening of the family in mind so that families can better instruct and disciple their children.[39]

---

[38] Bryan Nelson and Timothy Paul Jones, "The Problem and the Promise of Family Ministry," *Journal of Family Ministry* 1 (Fall-Winter 2010): 39.
[39] DeVries, 115.

We have already discussed the traditional youth ministry model which, in effect, removes young people from the influence of their parents as much as possible and instead entrusts a youth minister with their spiritual formation. This model is *absolutely foreign* to what the Bible presents in its descriptions of how faith is passed on to young people.[40] Family ministry, on the other hand, is an inherently biblical concept: "in many ways, family-based youth ministry is not a new model as much as it is a radical return to God's original design" for how young people should be raised in faith.[41]

Many verses in both the Old and New Testaments show the important role that parents and families play in the spiritual formation of children:

"And when your children say to you, 'What do you mean by this service?' you shall say, 'It is the sacrifice of the LORD's Passover, for he passed over the houses of the people of Israel in Egypt, when he struck the Egyptians but spared our houses.'" And the people bowed their heads and worshiped.

(Exodus 12.26-27, ESV)

Here, in the instruction of how to celebrate the Passover, parents are told that they need to use that opportunity to pass on to their kids the great story of how God saved his people from Egypt.

Perhaps the single most foundational biblical text for family ministry is the *Shema*, which offers a guide to parents for communicating the faith to their children:

Hear O Israel. The LORD our God, the LORD is One. You shall love the LORD your God with all your heart and with all your soul and with all your might. And these words that I command you today shall be on your heart. You shall teach them

---

[40] Ibid., 162, "For most Christian teenagers, Sunday school and youth group have become a substitute for spiritual training in the home."

[41] Ibid., 163.

diligently to your children, and shall talk of them when you sit in your house, and when you walk by the way, and when you lie down, and when you rise.

(Deuteronomy 6.4-7, ESV)

In context, Moses is sharing the Law with the people of Israel, and he makes it clear that parents have a responsibility to model faith at home. This modeling is an ongoing, constant process, and emphasizes that parents are supposed to teach their children about God's commandments by faithfully observing them through their daily behavior.[42]

There is another relevant passage in the Book of Joel:

Tell your children of it, and let your children tell their children, and their children to another generation.

(Joel 1.3, ESV)

Here, Joel is speaking about the prophetic message that God has given him, and he tells the people to whom he is prophesying that this message should be passed on to their children and grandchildren. Although the context here is specific, the general principle still applies: parents have the responsibility to share God's message with their kids.

Moving on to the New Testament, "the earliest Christians were converts from Judaism, and the center of Jewish religious life (particularly after the destruction of temple A.D. 70) was the home, not the synagogue."[43] Paul

---

[42] Mona DeKoven Fishbane, "'Honor Thy Father and Thy Mother': Intergenerational Spirituality and Jewish Tradition," in *Spiritual Resources in Family Therapy,* ed. Froma Walsh (New York: Guilford Press, 1999), 136; Stuart Win, "How Far Is Too Far? Segregation versus Integration in Youth Ministry," *St. Mark's Review* 225, no. 3 (2013): 129. Speaking of these verses, C. Ellis Nelson, "Spiritual Formation: A Family Matter," *Journal of Family Ministry* 20 (Fall 2006): 17, states, "Children absorb what their parents do and say. If their parents pray and try to lead a God-centered life, their children attempt to do likewise."

[43] Bridget M. Meehan, "Family-Centered Intergenerational Religious Education: Families Minister to Families." *Military Chaplains' Review* (1989): 41.

conveys this perspective in Ephesians 6.4:

Fathers, do not provoke your children to anger, but bring them up in the discipline and instruction of the Lord.

(Ephesians 6.4, ESV)

This verse emphasizes that "...God has called parents—and particularly fathers—to function as primary faith-trainers in their children's lives."[44]

There are other verses we could look at, including the qualification that elders or deacons must be good managers of their households (1 Timothy 3.4-5, 12; Titus 1.6) and direct commands to children (Ephesians 6.1; Colossians 3.20-21), but I think these are sufficient to illustrate that Scripture teaches that parents are supposed to teach their kids about God—who He is, what He has done, and what He wants us to do.[45]

A youth ministry that recognizes and emphasizes the vital role parents play in raising their children in the faith is more faithful to biblical teaching, and because of the great influence that parents have on their children, is likely to be more successful as well.[46]

None of that is to minimize the teaching and instruction that the church provides for young people. Certainly it is a great thing to have Bible classes at church, and it is good for young people to be exposed to sermons, have devotionals from the Bible, and go to events where they have the opportunity to hear speakers and teachers. The point here is that all of that should be *extra*.

---

[44] Robert L. Plummer, "Bring Them Up in the Discipline and Instruction of the Lord," *Journal of Family Ministry* 1 (Fall-Winter 2010): 21.

[45] For a comprehensive list of Bible verses which speak to the idea of family ministry, see Appendix A, pages 75-85.

[46] Powell and Clark, 69-92, spend an entire chapter on the idea that parents who communicate their faith at home greatly increase the likelihood that their children will have a faith that lasts.

It should be *additional* instruction to what young people are already receiving at home from the teaching and the example of their parents.

I want to speak directly to parents now: what you teach your kids and how you train them *matters*. As we discussed in the last chapter, research overwhelmingly indicates that parents are the *primary spiritual influencers* of their children. You don't simply have more influence over your kids than I do as their youth minister, or than the church does; you have more influence over them than *any group* does.[47] Practically speaking, what that means is that if you make it a priority to pass your faith on to your kids, chances are, they will get it. If you don't, it will be much harder for them to be faithful.[48]

As a parent, the most important thing you can do for your kids is to *teach* them about God and *show* them what it means to follow Him. As one author said, "In the end, awakening faith does not depend on how hard we press young people to love God, but on how much we show them that we do."[49]

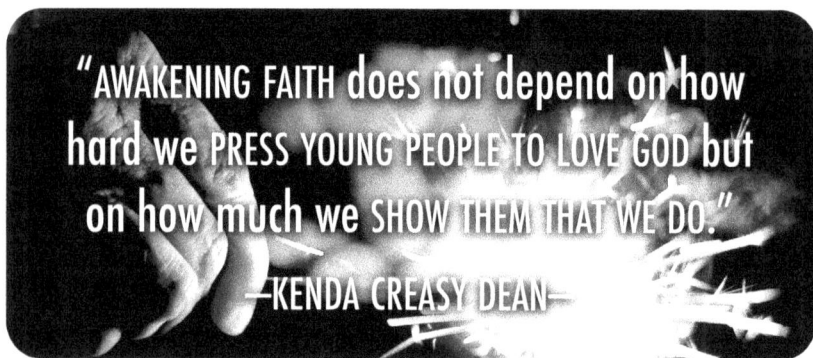

"AWAKENING FAITH does not depend on how hard we PRESS YOUNG PEOPLE TO LOVE GOD but on how much we SHOW THEM THAT WE DO."
—KENDA CREASY DEAN—

[47] Kenda Creasy Dean, *Almost Christian: What the Faith of Our Teenagers Is Telling the American Church* (Oxford: Oxford University Press, 2010): 18.

[48] Christian Smith with Melinda Lundquist Denton, *Soul Searching: The Religious and Spiritual Lives of American Teenagers* (Oxford: Oxford University Press, 2005): 262, states that when it comes to religious outcomes, young people will closely resemble their parents.

[49] Dean, 120.

From the perspective of Youth In Family Ministry, this means that we want to do things to *help* parents train their children in the faith rather than *prevent* them from doing so. There are three keys principles to follow to help parents disciple their kids:

(1) We want to enable parents to worship with their kids. I am not condemning children's church, and I think there are some ways to do it that are healthier than others (so if your congregation has some form of children's church, I'm not trying to offend you!). Having gotten that disclaimer out of the way, I am not a fan of the concept of children's church, and this is exactly the reason why.

I have an awesome, beautiful little girl who seems to think that worship is a great time for her to be as loud as she possibly can be. That is frustrating to my wife and I, and I understand that a lot of families with young children have similar struggles. Corralling kids can certainly be a distraction, and the concern that your child is distracting the worship experience of others is no fun either.

But as nice as it would be for children to be off somewhere being taken care of so parents can pay closer attention in worship, it is *more important* for children to watch their parents worship, sit alongside them as they worship, and learn to worship God themselves.

(2) We want to provide opportunities to live the Christian life as a family. I mentioned earlier that some congregations have the problem where they are constantly scheduling activities that pull people away from their families. I think it is a good thing for churches to stay busy. In Acts, we read accounts of the early church meeting together every day, and I think we should spend a lot of time with our faith families.

Having said that, as we spend time with our faith families—our church congregations—we need to also be able to spend time with our physical families in that context. So, a lot of events on our church calendar are specifically designed to allow physical families to be together to serve and fellowship as a part of our faith family.

(3) We want to help parents teach and raise their kids in the Lord.

If the job of parents is to pass on their faith to their kids, then a big part of our youth ministry should be to help parents do just that.[50]

In our youth ministry, this has involved things like combined Bible classes with teens and their parents, where teens and parents can learn alongside one another and also learn *from* one another. We also have had marriage classes and have plans for a parenting class

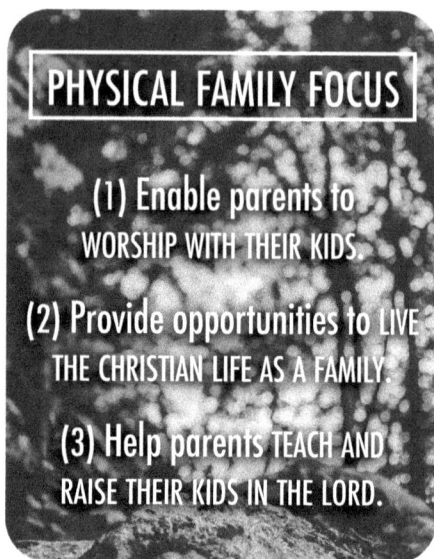

PHYSICAL FAMILY FOCUS

(1) Enable parents to WORSHIP WITH THEIR KIDS.

(2) Provide opportunities to LIVE THE CHRISTIAN LIFE AS A FAMILY.

(3) Help parents TEACH AND RAISE THEIR KIDS IN THE LORD.

in the future in order to help strengthen our families and better equip them to disciple their children.

And as a youth minister, I spend a lot of time working directly with the parents of my teens and trying to help them navigate through various issues that arise as they try to parent their children through difficult years. In general, instead of being some sort of surrogate parent who takes over the

---

[50] Win, 133: "Churches should consider how they will resource and affirm parents in their role as primary disciplers of youth. In some ways, this might be thought of as the primary purpose of youth ministry. See also Dorothy Jean Furnish, "Rethinking Children's Ministry," in *Rethinking Christian Education: Explorations in Theory and Practice,* ed. David S. Schuller (St. Louis: Chalice Press, 1993), 77-78.

job of discipling young people, I try to be more of a consultant to help parents do that job.

The Faith Family

As previously mentioned, the second major pillar of Youth In Family Ministry is the faith family, or church congregation.

In addition to the importance of parents and the physical family unit, over the last several years, youth ministry experts have increasingly come to recognize the importance of all generations of the church congregation in ministry to young people. This phenomenon is referred to as "intergenerational ministry" or "intergenerationality." Typically, these terms include the following ideas:

- Several representatives of multiple generations are present in church activities.

- Those present are engaged in mutual activities where genuine interaction is involved rather than just a one-sided lecturing format.[51]

- Activities include a wide range of spiritual experiences such as worship, service, fellowship, and outreach.

- The ultimate purpose of intergenerational activities is spiritual growth and development.[52]

---

[51] Brenda Snailum, "Integrating Intergenerational Ministry Strategies into Existing Youth Ministries: What can a Hybrid Approach be Expected to Accomplish?" *The Journal of Youth Ministry* 11, no. 2 (2013): 8, carefully explains the difference between "intergenerational" and "multigenerational": "It is important to emphasize that *mutually influential* relationships are the distinguishing characteristic of *intergenerational* community. In contrast, *multigenerational* settings are those social environments in which several generations are in proximity with each other but not necessarily in relationship."

[52] Holly Catterton Allen, "Guest Editorial: Bringing The Generations Back Together: Introduction To Intergenerationality," *Christian Education Journal*, 3rd ser., 9 (Spring 2012): 102.

We've already seen how Scripture emphasizes the important role of the physical family when it comes to raising young people in the faith; if anything, the Bible places an even greater emphasis on the importance of the faith family.[53] Perhaps that is not surprising, considering the way Jesus radically redefined who we should consider our primary family to be. According to Him, our ultimate family relationships should be determined not by flesh and blood, but by shared faith in God and obedience to Him (Matthew 12.46-50).[54]

Here is a sampling of what the Bible says about the importance of the faith family, whether the faith family in question is the Israelite people in the Old Testament, or the church in the New Testament:

Assemble the people, men, women, and little ones, and the sojourner within your towns, that they may hear and learn to fear the LORD your God, and be careful to do all the words of this law, and that their children, who have not known it, may hear and learn to fear the LORD your God as long as you live in the land that you are going over the Jordan to possess.

(Deuteronomy 31.12-13, ESV)

Here, Moses speaks the Law to the people of Israel and tells them to gather all the people, including the "little ones" and "children," so that they could hear and learn to fear the Lord. It was something for the entire congregation of Israel, the entire faith family, to do together.

---

[53] Win, 131: "Undoubtedly the separation from the wider Church, observable in many contemporary youth ministries, is unbiblical."

[54] See also the insightful commentary by Ben Witherington III, *Conflict & Community in Corinth: A Socio-Rhetorical Commentary on 1 & 2 Corinthians*, (Grand Rapids, Eerdmans, 1995), 180, n. 40: "What is desperately needed and seldom found in the church is an adequate theology of the family of faith. Paul believes that being brother sand sisters in Christ and sons and daughters of God transcends all other loyalties and should transform all other social relationships. Blood should not be thicker than the baptismal waters of the church."

Later, Joshua has a similar experience with the people of Israel:

And afterward he read all the words of the law, the blessing and the curse, according to all that is written in the Book of the Law. There was not a word of all that Moses commanded that Joshua did not read before all the assembly of Israel, and the women, and the little ones, and the sojourners who lived among them.

(Joshua 8.34-35, ESV)

In this context, Joshua is renewing the covenant with the people of Israel, and he does the same thing as Moses, making sure that all the people, including the "little ones," are present. It was the entire community together that had a covenant relationship with God.

The Book of Psalms contains multiple references to the intergenerational aspect of the faith family passing on their faith to those who are younger:

So even to old age and gray hairs, O God, do not forsake me, until I proclaim your might to another generation, your power to all those to come.

(Psalm 71.18, ESV)

Give ear, O my people, to my teaching; incline your ears to the words of my mouth! I will open my mouth in a parable; I will utter dark sayings from of old, things that we have heard and known, that our fathers have told us. We will not hide them from their children, but tell to the coming generation the glorious deeds of the LORD, and his might, and the wonders that he has done.

(Psalm 78.1-4, ESV)

In these passages the Psalmist expresses his desire to tell the next generation about the greatness of God. Within the family of faith, it is the responsibility of those who are older to tell the great things God has done to those who are younger.

The same idea is found in the New Testament, where the faith family is the church:

Older men are to be sober-minded, dignified, self-controlled, sound in faith, in love, and in steadfastness. Older women likewise are to be reverent in behavior, not slanderers or slaves to much wine. They are to teach what is good, and so train the young women to love their husbands and children.

(Titus 2.2-4, ESV)

Here Paul gives Titus specific instructions on what our relationships should be like in the church, and how older Christians are to serve as examples and teachers to those who are younger. Elsewhere, in 1 Timothy, Paul explains to Timothy the other side of the intergenerational coin:

Let no one despise you for your youth, but set the believers an example in speech, in conduct, in love, in faith, in purity.

(1 Timothy 4.12, ESV)

Paul tells young Timothy that by his good living, he can set an example for others to follow as well. So one of the benefits of living in community as a faith family is that we can learn from one another, regardless of age.

These verses are representative of how the Bible teaches that in the church, as a faith family, we all share in the responsibility of collectively raising our children in the Lord. Scripture teaches that it is the job of the entire faith family to be good stewards of God's kids and to help pass faith in Jesus Christ onto them.[55]

In addition to being thoroughly *biblical*, youth ministry that emphasizes the importance of the faith family and brings multiple generations together has proven to be particularly *effective* as well. Researchers and ministry leaders suggest many benefits of intergenerational ministry for the congregation including:

---

[55] For a comprehensive list of Bible verses which speak to the idea of the importance of the faith family in raising children in the Lord, see Appendix A.

- God's intention that faith be shared communally and from generation to generation is honored.
- The church is taught to value older adults.
- Special relationships between adults and youth are created.
- The strengths of one generation are used to meet the needs of another.
- Good role models are made available for children and teenagers.
- People's identification and feeling of belonging with the congregation is enhanced.[56]

These benefits directly relate to the problem of age segregation. When youth ministries intentionally provide opportunities for interaction between young people and the rest of the faith family, the number and quality of relationships that young people have with adult Christians increases, which in turn strengthens their identity as part of the church and tends to lead to a faith that lasts for life.[57]

We talked earlier about how many youth ministries do a lot of things to separate young people from the rest of the church as much as possible. In the Youth In Family Ministry Model we don't want to do that—we want the ties between our young people and the rest of the church to be as strong as possible. That leads to two key principles:

(1) We want to encourage relationships between young people and older, mature Christians. The more relationships that kids have with mature, adult Christians, the more likely it is that they will stay connected to

---

56 Roberto, 106-07. Christine M. Ross, "Four Congregations That Practice Intergenerationality," *Christian Education Journal,* 3rd ser., 9 (Spring 2012): 142, reports that in the congregations she studied that emphasized the faith family in their youth ministry, there was a decrease in the isolation of youth and an increase in understanding and unity within the congregation.

57 Black, 27.

the church. That's true for all kids, but especially for those who come from homes where their parents are not faithful Christians. For those children, the faith family needs to help stand in the gap by providing role models—people who love them and care for them and show the love of God and the Way of Jesus.[58]

We try to do this in a lot of ways. We have **adult mentors** who work directly with our students in small groups. We have many people who serve as **Bible class teachers** and get to know our students through that ministry. We have adult Christians who get to know our students by **hosting youth events,** going on trips as **chaperones**, and serving as **counselors at summer camp**.

I mentioned earlier that we have a lot of events on our church calendar at Farmington; many of those events are not just designed to let *physical* families spend time with one another, but also to let the entire *faith* family spend time with one another in service and fellowship. These are invaluable opportunities for relationships to develop between young people and mature Christians, and these relationships are a key part to helping our students develop a lasting faith.[59] We are always on the lookout for ways to strengthen relationships between our children and teens and more mature Christians.

(2) We want to remove young people from worshiping with the rest of the congregation as little as possible. If you want your kids to have a faith that will last beyond high school, research shows that one of the most

---

[58] Earlier, we discussed the great influence that parents have on their children. Research also shows that non-parental adults, "those in their faith communities who have reached out to them and built meaningful personal relationships with them," can have great influence on the lives of young people, Allen and Ross, 56.

[59] Allen and Ross, 126: "Religious belief and commitment are highly dependent upon the extent to which an individual is integrated into a religious community."

direct factors in this is the frequency with which they attend the worship services of the church.[60]

With that in mind, I want the kids in our congregation present for worship as frequently as possible! As a youth group, we are only absent from Sunday morning worship two Sundays per year, and one of those is when we are at a youth leadership convention with a significant percentage of our congregation. When we go to weekend youth rallies, it is our standard practice to return home Saturday night in order to be present for Sunday worship. On Sunday nights, once per month we travel to a small, rural congregation where our young men have an opportunity to help lead in worship. Beyond that, we are rarely gone from worship as a group. That is intentional, because we believe that it is vitally important for our young people to be at worship with our faith family. It lets them see how significant corporate worship is to a life of faith, and it glues them to the church.

> **FAITH FAMILY FOCUS**
>
> (1) ENCOURAGE RELATIONSHIPS between YOUNG PEOPLE and OLDER, MATURE CHRISTIANS.
>
> (2) REMOVE young people from WORSHIP with the REST OF THE CHURCH AS LITTLE AS POSSIBLE.

Speaking directly to parents again, there is something I want you to know, and I say this as lovingly but as earnestly as I can. If your family chooses to participate in worship only on Sunday mornings, or for whatever reason chooses to travel or be absent from Sunday worship a dozen or two dozen times per year or more, you greatly reduce the impact and influence the church can have on your kids, and you greatly weaken the bonds that tie your kids to the church!

---

[60] Powell and Clark, 97.

> **REGULAR ABSENCE from worship REDUCES the INFLUENCE the church can have on your kids and WEAKENS the BONDS that tie your kids to the church.**

The Bottom Line

In the early 2000s, a massive research study was conducted called the National Study of Youth and Religion (NSYR) that examined the spiritual lives of American teenagers. One of the key findings of that study is that, in young people, spiritual formation occurs in two places: *individual family households* and *multigenerational religious congregations.*[61] This research is helpful, but ultimately, all it tells us is something we should have already known if we were paying close attention to our Bibles: the physical family and the faith family are vitally important when it comes to passing faith on to young people. And that is why those two units form the basis of Youth In Family Ministry.

Questions For Reflection

1. What are some ways in which Scripture emphasizes the importance of the *physical family* in passing faith in God on to young people?

2. What are some ways in which Scripture emphasizes the importance of the *faith family* in passing faith in God on to young people?

3. Is it surprising that something as basic as church attendance has such a major impact on long-term faithfulness in young people? Why or why not?

---

[61] Christian Smith with Patricia Snell, *Souls in Transition: The Religious and Spiritual Lives of Emerging Adults* (Oxford: Oxford University Press, 2009): 286, "These are the two crucial contexts of...religious formation in the United States. If formation does not happen here, it will—with rare exceptions—not happen anywhere."

Putting Philosophy Into Practice

Now that we have established the biblical basis for the physical family and the faith family as the primary means for raising young people in faith, we want to get very practical. How do we take these ideas and actually implement them in the local church? How do we re-envision the work we do in youth ministry to emphasize the importance of the physical and faith families?

To reiterate some ideas from the previous chapter, "family ministry" usually refers to ministry practices that emphasize the importance and priority of the physical family in discipling young people, and "intergenerational ministry" usually refers to ministry practices that emphasize the entire congregation being together and teaching and learning from one another. In the Youth In Family Ministry model, the physical and faith family pillars sum up both of those values. As you can imagine—and as we will see—there is a great deal of overlap between these two ideas, and so the process of implementing a Youth

In Family Ministry in a local congregation will weave both of these concepts together.[62]

Step One: Establish Youth In Family Ministry as a Core Value

Youth In Family Ministry is not just another program to add to a long list of programs that your church has already. Rather, it is a value that should affect all the programs of the local congregation.

In other words, in order for Youth In Family Ministry to be effective, it must be more than just a fad or a method; it needs to become a core value that the congregation understands and deeply cares about.[63] Making a new idea a core value in your congregation is easier said than done, but there are several things that you can do to help bring that about. Below are some suggestions for different things I have tried in my ministry context to try to get people to buy into the Youth In Family concept. Obviously some of these ideas would vary from one church to another depending on the way you do things and depending on what your role is within the congregation or youth ministry.

---

[62] In fact, Mark DeVries, *Family-Based Youth Ministry*, Rev. ed. (Downers Grove, IL: InterVarsity Press, 2004), sees family ministry and intergenerational ministry as two sides of the same coin, devoting one chapter to the importance of the nuclear family, 59-69, and then another to the significance of what he calls the "extended Christian family", 83-95. Many of his suggestions deal with both of these areas. I appreciate DeVries's approach, as my research has repeatedly revealed the close ties between intergenerational and family youth ministry and the desperate need for both in youth ministry today. My ideas closely resemble and follow his. Brenda Snailum, "Implementing Intergenerational Youth Ministry," 168-75, and John Roberto, "Our Future Is Intergenerational," *Christian Education Journal* 3rd ser., 9 (Spring 2012): 111-17, provide much of the structure of the following plan through their respective proposals.

[63] Snailum, 168-69.

One of the first things I did was to develop a ministry plan with all of these ideas (in fact, that ministry plan was the original kernel of the book you are now reading), and to present that to a lot of the **key leaders** of our congregation. I shared it with our preaching minister so he could be aware of what we are trying to accomplish. I shared it with our shepherds, and especially talked through it in detail with our shepherd who specifically focuses on the young people of our congregation. I shared the plan with our youth deacons, so they would understand the direction in which we were moving. Finally, I shared these ideas with our ministry leader over involvement, so church activities could be planned with the Youth In Family concept in mind. It took a lot of work and a lot of conversations to get the word around, but this was an important step. You will not be able to implement the Youth In Family Model as a core value unless the leaders of your congregation understand it and are on board.

Also, I **preached a sermon** on a Sunday morning in which I discussed the Youth In Family Ministry philosophy. I shared a lot of the same material that you have read in this book, ranging from the problems we have with young people leaving the church after high school to what the Bible teaches about the physical family and the faith family being the key ingredients in raising young people in the Lord. I got a tremendous response from the congregation after that lesson, and it was a helpful tool to let people understand the biblical foundation beneath what we are trying to accomplish in our youth ministry. My only regret is that I wish I would have preached that sermon a lot sooner!

Third, we offered a **combined teen and parent class** where we studied the book *Sticky Faith: Everyday Ideas To Build Lasting Faith In Your Kids.*[64] This is a book that heavily emphasizes the importance of parental involvement and intergenerational relationships at church in the spiritual formation of teens, and has been very influential to me as a youth minister. We studied Sticky Faith together for a quarter, with parents and teens learning side by side and from one another as we talked about ways in which we could all work together to develop a faith that lasts for life. It was a very successful study, and we have actually repeated it since first doing it three years ago. After all, since Youth In Family Ministry is a core value, these ideas need to be continually reinforced.

Finally, even **within our youth group,** I have emphasized these principles to our students at different times and in different ways. Recently our youth group theme for the school year was "Church Family," and in our Wednesday night Bible class we focused on how the church is like a family and ways in which we can strengthen those ties. And I can tell that they're starting to get it: one young lady in our group recently told me about how she had visited another church with a friend, and at that church, the youth group was separated into its own building and the teens never saw the adults or the rest of the congregation. She said that she thought it was "weird" and that it wasn't the way things should be! Those discussions on age segregation and the importance of the faith family are starting to sink in!

One word of warning: the process of establishing Youth In Family Ministry as a core value is not something you can do overnight. In our congregation, it

[64] Kara E. Powell and Chap Clark, *Sticky Faith: Everyday Ideas to Build Lasting Faith in Your Kids* (Grand Rapids: Zondervan, 2011). I am indebted to Joseph Horton, current pulpit minister and former youth minister of the Winchester Church of Christ in Winchester, TN, for pointing me to *Sticky Faith,* and also for his guidance on our combined teen and parent class.

has taken the better part of three years and some people still aren't quite on board yet...but a lot of people are starting to get it!

Step Two: Take Advantage of Already-Existing Programs

Generally speaking, people struggle with rapid and significant change, and even if you are bringing about positive changes for good reasons, it is possible to do that in an unhealthy way. The *last* thing you want to do in trying to bring your church's youth ministry more in line with biblical principles is to sabotage that effort by trying to accomplish too much change too quickly!

With this in mind, I think it is very important that you take a look at the programs and activities that your congregation *already has in place* and look at how those programs and activities can be tweaked to make them more family-friendly and intergenerational in nature rather than implementing a host of brand new activities to which the congregation must adjust.[65] In fact, one author suggests that you not add more than one new program per year, and even that you avoid using terms like "family ministry" or "intergenerational" to describe your new programs until these ideas represent a core value that everyone in your congregation understands.[66] In other words, don't make a big deal about how you're changing everything and starting something new and different. Instead, simply make alterations to what is already going on at your church and bring those things more in line with Youth In Family values.

When I examined a lot of the things that we were already doing at the church in Farmington, I realized that there were a number of activities and programs that, with minor adjustments, would provide excellent

---

[65] Snailum, 170-72. Jolene L. Roehlkepartain, "Innovative Ways to Build an Effective Family Ministry," *Journal of Family Ministry* 15 (Winter 2001): 18.

[66] DeVries, 177-81.

opportunities for families and the church as a whole to work together to disciple our young people. By taking advantage of these already-existing programs, I was able to emphasize the Youth In Family Ministry values that we see in Scripture without jarring people with a lot of change.

I'll share examples of some of those activities and programs in the next section.

Step Three: Provide a Variety of Youth In Family Activities

If Youth In Family Ministry is to truly be a core value of the church, then a family focus (and by that I mean a focus on both the *physical family* and the *faith family*) needs to be present in all areas of church life. The following are some suggested practices in the areas of worship, service/outreach, education, mentoring, and fellowship.[67]

Since my goal in this chapter is to provide some practical ways to apply the ideas that we have talked about, I will share some examples of things that we have tried at Farmington, and also some other ideas that I have compiled from various sources.

Worship is one of the most significant areas for Youth In Family Ministry,[68] as it is perhaps the most visible and central practice of the church and also provides an environment where people of all generations are easily incorporated.

Earlier I discussed how I do not believe that children's church is ideal because of the way it removes kids from their physical and faith families during worship. At the same time, just because you *don't* have children's

---

[67] Roberto, 111.

[68] Powell and Clark, 97, 113-14. Roland D. Martinson, *Effective Youth Ministry: A Congregational Approach,* (Minneapolis: Augsburg Publishing House, 1988): 93-95.

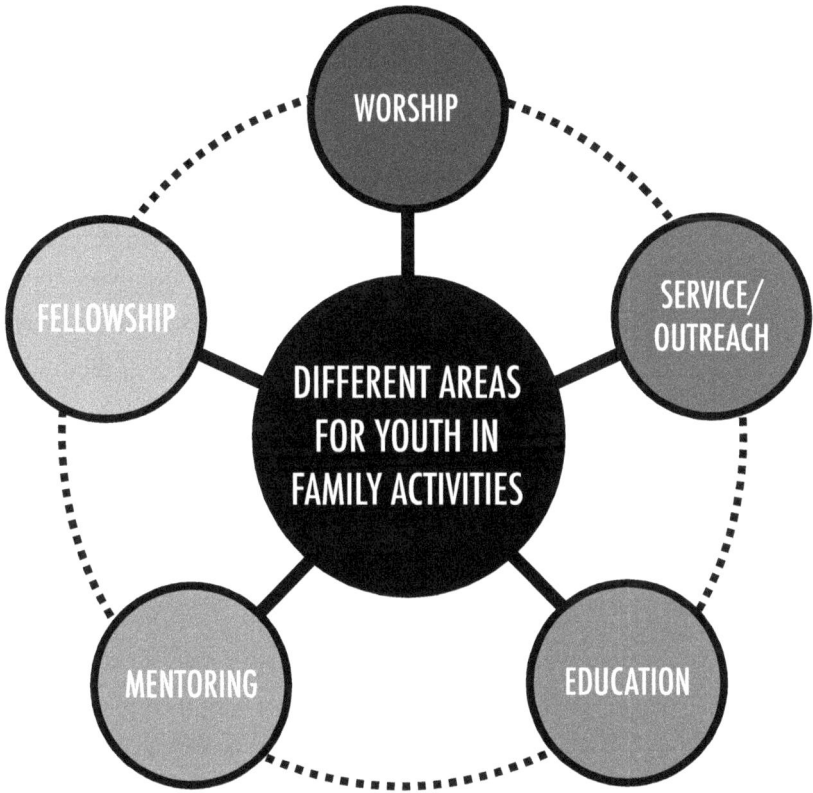

WORSHIP

SERVICE/
OUTREACH

FELLOWSHIP

DIFFERENT AREAS
FOR YOUTH IN
FAMILY ACTIVITIES

MENTORING

EDUCATION

church doesn't automatically guarantee that you are doing a good job of incorporating all ages into your congregational worship. In fact, the primary motivation for children's church in the first place arose from the realization that we often do *not* do a good job of including our young people in worship. So we need to do more than simply allow them to be present while we continue with (worship) business as usual.

On the other hand, including children in corporate worship doesn't mean that we have to dumb down every teaching and practice to the point that any toddler can understand it. Inevitably, this would leave many adults feeling very dissatisfied and spiritually malnourished on a perpetual diet of milk.[69]

---

[69] Harkness, "Intergenerational Corporate Worship," 17.

A better and more balanced viewpoint would be to acknowledge that we can include people of all ages in our congregational worship without *all* participants understanding *all* that is going on at *all* times.[70] Since the church is the family of God, using an example from a family context might be helpful to illustrate what I am talking about.[71] As a family sits around the table to eat dinner together, several conversations occur throughout the meal. Some conversations may include adults and children, while others are just between adults, and still others are just between children. No member of the family gets up and leaves the table if they do not understand something that is said or if a particular conversation is not directed at them. Similarly, in congregational worship, as long as all people—including children—are acknowledged and included at times, the progression of the faith family's worship can continue as naturally as a dinner conversation at home.

With all of that in mind, there are a variety of things that can be done to help young people grow spiritually through contact with their physical and faith families in worship:[72]

- An obvious starting point is to have all families and generations worship together, which is something that we do at Farmington. Young people see their parents and other adult Christians worship and learn that this is a valued part of the Christian life.

- To further support the idea of the importance of our entire church family worshiping together, our youth group is present for congregational worship as often as possible.

[70] Ibid.

[71] J. Tidwell, "The Child in the Church," *Journal of Christian Education Papers* 64 (1979): 23, quoted in Harkness, "Intergenerational Corporate Worship," 17, is the source of this "family conversation" illustration.

[72] Furnish, 82-83, provides an excellent list of suggestions for developing intergenerational worship.

- Young men are regularly involved in public worship, and one Sunday night per month, we have Youth-Led Worship, where our youngest boys through high school students lead songs and prayers, read Scripture, serve the Lord's Supper, and present short Bible lessons.

- Our singing service is geared toward multiple generations as well, as the songs that we sing are a balanced mixture of traditional favorites and contemporary songs. Recognizing that we have a variety of people of all different ages, we try to sing a variety of songs.

- Since both parents and children worship together and hear the same sermon each week, we started including "Table Talk" questions each week in our church bulletin. These are intended to be a take-home resource for parents to use to discuss the morning's lesson as they sit around the table to have Sunday dinner together.

- Invite older children to serve as ushers or greeters who make guests feel welcome and help them to find a place to sit.

- Encourage children to take part in the offering. Not only does this include them in the worship of the church, it also teaches them of the importance of giving back to God, and being a part of the financial work of the church.

- Edit some of the vocabulary (i.e. "church words") that is used in the course of the worship service, and explain what is going on. Not only will this help children and young people understand what is happening, it will also be beneficial to those who are visiting.[73]

---

[73] For example, before observing the Lord's Supper, explain what it is. If you have an Invitation Song, explain what people are being "invited" to do. In the sermon, do not use words like "sanctification" or "justification" without explaining what they mean.

- Make sure that some of the sermon illustrations used during the preaching are taken from the experiences of children, to help connect them to what is being said.

Service/Outreach is another area where parents and other mature Christians can model what a life of discipleship looks like for their children. Jesus modeled these values for His disciples, taking the form of a servant during His life on earth and always keeping the mission of seeking and saving the lost foremost in His mind and activities. Just as Jesus strove to help his disciples develop a mature faith, we too want to reinforce these same characteristics.

Here are some of the things we have done and some of the ideas we have for allowing our physical families and faith families to work together in these areas:

- Each spring our congregation has a Day of Service where we divide into groups and go out into the community to perform a variety of service projects—wash cars, mow lawns, fix up flowerbeds at schools, pick up garbage, etc. This was an event that we had participated in for a couple of years, but to bring it more in line with a Youth In Family perspective, we simply changed the ways we split up our work crews. Rather than divide the crews by age and have all of the young people working together on one project, we now spread our young people out across different work groups and they serve with adults. Some work alongside their parents. This is a good example of taking an already-existing program and tweaking it to make it more family-friendly and intergenerational in nature (see Step Two above).

- We have a group of older women who get together and make quilts for Arkansas Children's Hospital and others who need them. At times, we have had some of our younger girls come and spend time with these mature Christian ladies, learning how to quilt and how to serve.

• For years, many adults in our congregation would "adopt" less-fortunate children from our school district and buy Christmas presents for them, and our youth group would do the same thing. Eventually it occurred to us that rather than having two separate but parallel activities, why not have one big, combined event? Now, each year our congregation adopts a bunch of children, we all meet together at the church building, group kids and teens with adults (often with adults who are not their own parents), load up the bus, head to Wal-Mart to shop and then come back to our building to wrap presents and share a meal together. We call it the "Elf Party" (because we are Santa's helpers) and it is a blast—one of the best things we do all year.

• Mission trips offer an outstanding opportunity for physical families and multiple generations of the faith family to work alongside one another in serving others and spreading the gospel together.[74] For the past two summers, our congregation has taken a foreign mission trip, and members of several generations (including children) have made the trip and been blessed by the opportunity to serve alongside one another on the mission field.

• For a few years, our youth group has supported the work of a Christian school in Malawi, Africa, and one year, they led our congregation in a school supply drive. They worked in the homes of several of our adult members, raking leaves, moving furniture, and doing other chores in exchange for donated school supplies that we sent to Africa.

---

[74] Allen and Ross, 227-38.

Education provides a tremendous opportunity for interaction between young people and adults *and* for equipping families to be the primary disciple-makers of their children:

- I mentioned this previously, but a while back we brought our teenagers and parents together and had a combined class based on the book *Sticky Faith*. This provided multiple generations with the opportunity to learn from and alongside one another. This was a great experience and we got a ton of positive feedback from the parents. The material in this book and the model of the class itself are both so foundational to what Youth In Family Ministry is all about that we have since repeated the class.

- Vacation Bible School is a big deal at our congregation, and our teenagers are heavily involved in every aspect of it. They work to set up and decorate in advance, they teach children's classes in costume, they run the puppet shows, they lead the classes from station to station, and they help tear down and clean up when everything is over. This emphasizes that intergenerationality happens in both directions, as young people can teach those who are even younger than they are, and helps to solidify relationships within the church.

- Some of our junior high and high school girls have rotated into some of our children's Bible classes for a few weeks at a time to assist teachers and learn how to teach themselves. This enables our young ladies to receive training from adult women while also spending time interacting with kids from our congregation.

- Dating relationships are a significant part of teenage life and adolescent development, and it is important that teenagers have a Christian perspective on dating. A neat way to talk about dating in Bible class in an intergenerational way would be to have older couples with long and successful marriages come into class and be interviewed as examples of mature relationships.

- Special seminars for parents on marriage, parenting, personal finance, and technology and social media use among teens would be beneficial as well. After all, *any training* that helps parents to model the Christian lifestyle for their children in a better way is an important part of Youth In Family Ministry.

Mentoring is a vital component of Youth In Family Ministry, and involves specifically pairing older Christians with those who are younger as a means of developing close relationships and illustrating what mature faith looks like.

In *Sticky Faith*, Kara Powell and Chap Clark argue that we need to develop a 5:1 adult-to-kid ratio where there are five adult Christians who show an interest in each student or child.[75] These are adults who intentionally invest in the lives of young people: speaking to them when they see them at worship, watching their ball games, sharing meals with them, etc. There are several things that we are involved in to try to encourage these sorts of mentoring relationships:

- We have recently begun a new program that I believe will turn out to be the best way that we mentor our students. On Wednesday nights we begin class in one large group to have announcements, sing a couple of songs, and have a short lesson, and then we split into our small groups, which are based on age and gender. Each small group is led by multiple adults from the congregation of different generations, and these small group leaders not only lead their group in further discussion of the lesson, but they also invest in the students

75 Powell and Clark, 101-21.

relationally. This means they get to know their students by interacting with them in class, but also by texting them, supporting them at extracurricular activities, and hanging out with them outside of the church setting.

- You may be familiar with youth leadership programs such as Lads to Leaders (L2L) or Leadership Training for Christ (LTC). At Farmington we are involved in L2L, and our program works on a mentor basis, as each student participant has an adult mentor that he or she works with. From that starting point, we have been working to extend those relationships throughout the year and expand their focus beyond L2L events. Mentors help their students prepare for the L2L Convention, but beyond that, they work to build relationships with their students, show them that they care for them, and provide a mature Christian example for them.

- Each year at our youth group winter retreat, the whole retreat is formatted so that our students are divided into small discussion groups led by an adult mentor in an effort to provide structured student-adult interaction. This has been successful each year we have done it and has led to closer ties between our students and the adults involved.

- Since we know that the years immediately after high school are a particularly challenging time for young people, we started an "Adopt a Grad" program where people from our congregation "adopt" those who have graduated from high school, sending them care packages, texting them, and taking them out for meals.

- Another fun activity we tried in our Wednesday night youth group class several months ago was called "Meet the Family." Our youth group students randomly drew cards with the picture and name of a person or married couple from our church directory, and then the student had to go and meet the person on the card and sit down to talk to them, interview them, and then come back and report to the rest of the class about the people they have met. This was simply an effort to force our teens outside of their comfort zones a bit and make connections with older Christians.

Fellowship activities can easily be structured to promote Youth In Family Ministry as well:

- At Farmington, we have a significant number of congregation-wide fellowship meals—if "potluck" can be used as an adjective, then we are the potluckiest church I have ever seen! These meals provide an excellent opportunity for interaction between all age groups.

- Each Fall, we have our Family Retreat. By "family," I mean it is for our entire church family, and this will be a great opportunity for us to get away, pray, study, fellowship, and play together as a faith family. Retreats like this are a great opportunity for families to have fun and learn together as well.[76]

- At different times throughout the year, we have church-wide Fall Festivals, Trunk or Treats, Memorial Day Cookouts, etc., with carnival games and activities for families.

- One idea that we have had for an event that illustrates the principle that older Christians can also learn from younger ones would be to hold a technology tutorial. Teens (who have been around

---

[76] Carol Duerksen, *Building Together: Developing Your Blueprint for Congregational Youth Ministry* (Newton, KS: Faith & Life Resources, 2001): 70. Powell, *The Sticky Faith Guide For Your Family,* 67: "As a youth leader, I often tell families that a student who attends a weekend retreat experiences the relational equivalent of attending Sunday school for six months."

technology and smart phones their entire lives) could show older members how to operate their cell phones or how to set up and use social media accounts to keep in touch with extended family.

- Also, a game night for the entire faith family would provide a great opportunity for fellowship. Parents could partner up with their kids, or partners and teams could be assigned randomly among the congregation, regardless of age.

The key idea in all of this is that there are a lot of different types of activities in which we participate as the body of Christ. Because of that, we should seek to incorporate Youth In Family Ministry principles across the wide array of activities and programs the church is involved in: worship, service/outreach, education, mentoring, and fellowship.

Hopefully, this list of ideas has gotten you excited about all sorts of things you can try in your own church setting. One piece of advice before you plan out your entire church calendar of events: *it is a good idea to get a variety of people involved in the planning process.* If you want to have an intergenerational game night, make sure that you get input from people of different generations about games they want to play. If you want to make sure that the singing in your worship reaches *all* generations, seek feedback from teenagers, Baby Boomers, and 90-year olds. And if you want to plan a family retreat, make sure you talk to people with small kids or else you might inadvertently plan something that isn't very family-friendly at all.[77]

Another idea to keep in mind as you plan activities is that in order to really accomplish the goals of Youth In Family Ministry, you need to make sure that you are *actively promoting* interaction and the development of relationships

---

[77] Ellen Renee Dill, "Planning for All Ages: Intergenerational Events Can Build Bridges in a Church," *The Christian Ministry* 17, no. 2 (March 1986): 17.

between parents and their children or people of different generations. For example, it is not enough to have a congregational meal where four different generations are present if those generations do not actually interact with one another. When given the choice, people will naturally gravitate toward others who are like them, so it is important that you plan activities and events in such a way that people are forced to interact with each other and thereby build the relationships that you are seeking.

Step Four: Balance Physical and Faith Family Activities with Age-Specific Ministry

By this point, I hope you can see how important I think Youth In Family Ministry is: it reflects what the Bible teaches about raising our kids and it is very effective as well. But as important as Youth In Family Ministry is and as important as intergenerational and family activities are, they must be kept in balance with age-specific ministry.[78] As one youth ministry expert writes, "natural differences exist between generational groups in communities, and this fact cannot, and should not, be ignored."[79]

Youth in Family Ministry doesn't mean that you have seven year-olds come into the auditorium class for a study of Song of Solomon. It doesn't mean that you disband your youth group. It doesn't mean that you fire your youth minister (really, don't do that!).

In fact, the teenage years are absolutely crucial when it comes to a child's development, and during this period of life, our young people are surrounded by various pressures which can distract and discourage them from faithfully

---

[78] Snailum, 169.

[79] Allan G. Harkness, "Intergenerational and Homogenous-Age Education: Mutually Exclusive Strategies for Faith Communities?," *Religious Education,* 95, no. 1 (Winter 2000): 54.

PROVIDING BALANCE IN YOUTH IN FAMILY MINISTRY

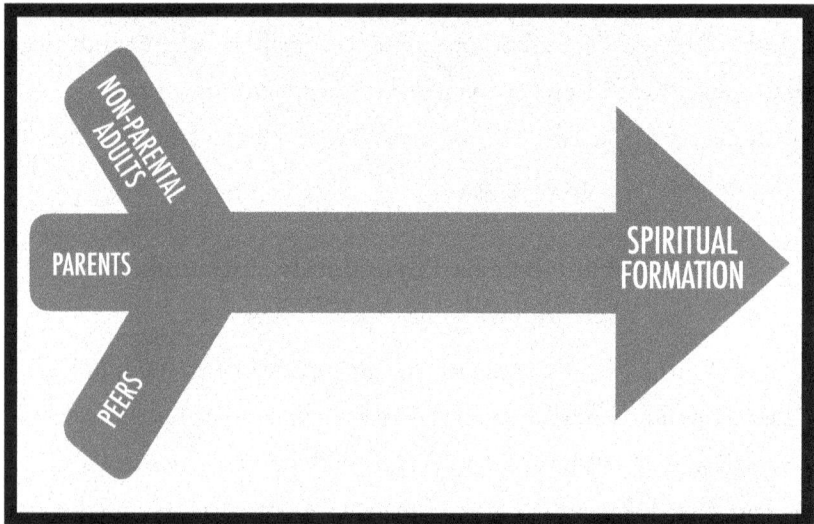

NON-PARENTAL ADULTS

PARENTS

PEERS

SPIRITUAL FORMATION

SOURCE: Brenda Snailum, "Integrating Intergenerational Ministry Strategies into Existing Youth Ministries: What can a Hybrid Approach be Expected to Accomplish?" The Journal of Youth Ministry 11, no. 2 (2013): 19-23

following Jesus Christ. This means that the teenage years are a time that requires special attention.

Furthermore, while we have rightly emphasized the huge influence that parents and other adults have on children, according to the National Study of Youth and Religion, after age twelve, the influence of parents decreases and the influence of peers, the media, music, and social media become more prevalent.[80] Thus, it is especially important that, in addition to providing opportunities for young people to be around their physical and faith families and benefit from meaningful relationships with mature Christian adults, we

---

[80] David Briggs, "The No. 1 Reason Teens Keep the Faith as Young Adults," *Huffington Post,* October 29, 2014, http://www.huffingtonpost.com/david-briggs/the-no-1-reason-teens-kee_b_6067838.html (accessed January 15, 2016).

also enable young people to establish relationships with Christian peers alongside whom they can learn and grow. The combination of these three streams of influence—parents, other adult Christians, and Christian peers—working together provides the best model for healthy spiritual formation in our young people.

With all of this in mind, we still have a youth group at Farmington. We still have Bible classes for different ages, and we continue to go to summer youth camps and take youth trips. These things are important. However, as you have already read, these age-specific activities and ministries are complemented by a host of activities which emphasize the importance of the physical and faith families in developing faith in our kids. Youth In Family Ministry is not an either/or approach; it's both/and. There is value to be had in age-specific ministry, and we want to recognize that. But the days of systematic age segregation are behind us; we're not interested in doing that anymore.

Step Five: Evaluate and Make Mid-Course Corrections

As you work to implement a Youth In Family Ministry model in your church, it is important that you constantly evaluate the process to see how things are going. We have tried to do this at the church in Farmington.

In fact, this is probably a good time to emphasize an important point: our Youth In Family Ministry at Farmington is not a finished product. We are always looking for new things to try out and better ways to enable our physical families and faith family to work together to raise our young people in the Lord. As you think about Youth In Family ministry in your church context and brainstorm about specific ways to put these principles into action, I would love to hear your ideas!

Making these transitions in your congregation is a process, and it is important to know up front that you will try things that do not work as well as you envision—some of them might even fail miserably! It is also important to make sure that your expectations are realistic. As this book has repeatedly emphasized, a youth ministry that properly emphasizes the physical family and the faith family as the primary spiritual influencers of young people is in line both with biblical teaching and the current research on how to best bring about lifelong faith in young people. Having said that, it is important to emphasize that the problem of young people leaving the church is a complex issue, and the Youth In Family Ministry model is not a guaranteed solution to that problem.[81]

What I *can* guarantee is that as you try to implement Youth In Family Ministry in your congregation, there will be some problems, and it will be important for you to evaluate the process and make corrections as you go.[82]

This is not a one-size-fits-all approach. Your congregational needs may mean that some of the activities above will need to be implemented differently or may not be beneficial at all. Some of the things that have worked great for us may not be ideal in your context. It is possible that for one reason or another, it will be necessary to follow these steps in a different order, or to add steps of your own. You may find that you immediately get buy-in from leaders in your church because this is a need that they already understand, but on the other hand, you may have to come up with even more ways than I have described here to emphasize these ideas to your leaders before they get it. You

---

[81] Snailum, "Integrating Intergenerational Ministry," 22: "It is important to remember that church attrition and related ills are multifaceted issues, and adopting an intergenerational ministry strategy may be only a part of the answer." For a partial list of some of the many reasons why young people leave the church, see pages 19-20.

[82] Dill, 17.

may put a lot of thought and planning into implementing a new intergenerational activity or program only for it to be a complete failure when you actually do it.

When these sorts of problems inevitably arise, don't get discouraged; instead, *try something else*! Ultimately, we are not trying to follow a rigid model; we *are* trying to be faithful to what Scripture teaches about how to raise our kids in such a way that they develop a mature faith that lasts throughout their lives. That will require us to take some risks and try things that may not be successful, but helping our young people stay faithful is worth it. We cannot afford to give up!

Questions For Reflection

1. In your context, what are the most effective actions you could take to establish Youth In Family Ministry as a core value?

2. What are some programs or activities your congregation is already involved in that could be tweaked to reflect more of a Youth In Family Ministry perspective?

3. What are one or two new programs or activities that could be implemented in your church that would strengthen your physical families or encourage interaction between the different generations of your faith family?

Conclusion

jesus loves the little children

A Repeated Scene

The gospel writers go out of their way to tell a similar story time and time again.[83] People bring their children to Jesus so that He can bless them. The disciples assume that kids are beneath the notice of a great rabbi, and so they try to turn them away, but Jesus rebukes the apostles and uses the situation as a teaching opportunity.

There are a few principles that we can glean from these situations:

- *Children are really important to Jesus.* In ancient cultures, children (especially sons) were valued as heirs, but generally speaking, they were not valued as individuals until they reached adulthood. The apostles thought that Jesus was too busy to be bothered by children, but Jesus turned that thinking on its head by stopping whatever He was doing and receiving the kids who were brought to Him. Clearly, Jesus thought that children were important and of great value.

---

[83] See Matthew 18.1-6; 19.13-15; Mark 9.35-37; 10.13-16; Luke 9.46-48; 18.15-17.

- *The kingdom of heaven belongs to children.* Repeatedly, Jesus makes the point that His disciples must become like little children in order to enter His kingdom. Just as children are vulnerable and trustingly dependent on their parents, so we as disciples of Jesus Christ need to acknowledge our ultimate helplessness and totally depend on our Heavenly Father. This is an especially counter-cultural message for those of us who live in a society that holds up self-sufficiency and independence as virtues to be emulated.[84] Instead of these values, Jesus says that citizens of the Kingdom should rely entirely upon the King.

- *Treating children well is connected to treating Jesus well.* As mentioned above, children did not occupy an enviable position in ancient cultures. They were the least important and least powerful members of their communities. Repeatedly, though, Jesus emphasizes the upside-down values of His kingdom, where those who give up their lives for His sake are saved, and those who humbly serve and welcome the weak and powerless are considered to be great. Furthermore, Jesus goes on to say that to welcome people like this, including children, is the same as welcoming Him and His Father.

These principles should cause us to pause and ask ourselves some important questions:

- *Do we treat our children like they are important to us?* In a society in which youth is idolized and parents often live vicariously through the athletic accomplishments of their kids, this may seem like

---

[84] Stephen W. Dixon, "What's So Special About Children? A Reconsideration of the Use Made of Scriptures such as Matthew 18:1-5 in Advocating the Importance of Children for the Church," *Journal of Childhood and Religion* 5, no. 1 (January 2014): 28, 33.

a ludicrous question at first, but hear me out. As parents, are we willing to interrupt our busy schedules, stop what we are doing, and deliberately focus on passing faith on to our kids? As a congregation, are we willing to alter the things we are doing in order to build lasting faith in our kids, even if it is harder and less efficient than outsourcing their spiritual training to a youth minister?

• *Do we include our children in God's kingdom?* It is common to hear well-meaning Christians talk about young people as the "church of tomorrow". I understand what is meant by that statement, and certainly we do want our children to be active leaders in the church of tomorrow. At the same time, I think it reveals some faulty thinking, because a key part of building faith in young people is for them to be active in the life of the church *now*. Do we enable and encourage our kids to be active in the worship, service, training, and fellowship of God's kingdom now, while they are young, or do we make them wait until they are adults before we include them?

• *Are we treating Jesus well by treating His children well?* No one likes to be accused of not treating their children well. Having said that, if, as a physical family and as a faith family, we are engaged in practices that make it less likely that our kids will develop a lifelong faith, can we really claim to be treating our children well? And based on the words of Jesus Himself, if we aren't treating our children well, what does that suggest about how we are treating Him?

All of this brings us back to a topic discussed way back at the beginning of this book: stewardship. Jesus' interactions with children in Scripture and the questions above call us to reflect upon our roles as stewards.

Remember, God has entrusted us—both in our physical families and in our church family—with *His* children. We tend to think of them as *ours,* but truly, ultimately, they are *His.* "Our" children belong to God.

It is my sincere hope that this book has helped you to see that clearly, and has shown how we can be faithful stewards of God's children through Youth In Family Ministry.

Appendix A

youth in family ministry in scripture

There are many, many passages in Scripture that emphasize that young people are important to God, and the central role of the physical family or the faith family in the task of passing faith on to them. Below is a collection of some of those passages.[85]

Old Testament

God also said to Moses, "Say this to the people of Israel, 'The LORD, the God of your fathers, the God of Abraham, the God of Isaac, and the God of Jacob, has sent me to you.' This is my name forever, and thus I am to be remembered throughout all generations."

(Exodus 3.15, ESV)

And when your children say to you, "What do you mean by this service?" you shall say, "It is the sacrifice of the LORD'S Passover, for he passed over the houses of the people of Israel in Egypt, when he struck the Egyptians but spared our houses." And the people bowed their heads and worshiped.

---

[85] This list of scriptures is based largely off a similar list in Allen and Ross, 294-307.

(Exodus 12.26-27, ESV)

Hear O Israel. The LORD our God, the LORD is One. You shall love the LORD your God with all your heart and with all your soul and with all your might. And these words that I command you today shall be on your heart. You shall teach them diligently to your children, and shall talk of them when you sit in your house, and when you walk by the way, and when you lie down, and when you rise.

(Deuteronomy 6.4-7, ESV)

And you shall rejoice before the LORD your God, you and your sons and your daughters, your male servants and your female servants, and the Levite that is within your towns, since he has no portion or inheritance with you.

(Deuteronomy 12.12, ESV)

All of you are standing today in the presence of the LORD your God—your leaders and chief men, your elders and officials, and all the other men of Israel, together with your children and your wives, and the foreigners living in your camps...You are standing here in order to enter into a covenant with the LORD your God.

(Deuteronomy 29.10-12, NIV)

Assemble the people, men, women, and little ones, and the sojourner within your towns, that they may hear and learn to fear the LORD your God, and be careful to do all the words of this law, and that their children, who have not known it, may hear and learn to fear the LORD your God as long as you live in the land that you are going over the Jordan to possess.

(Deuteronomy 31.12-13, ESV)

And afterward he read all the words of the law, the blessing and the curse, according to all that is written in the Book of the Law. There was not a word of all that Moses commanded that Joshua did not read before all the assembly of Israel, and the women, and the little ones, and the sojourners who lived among them.

(Joshua 8.34-35, ESV)

Therefore he said, "Let us now build an altar, not for burnt offering, nor for sacrifice, but to be a witness between us and you, and between our generations after us, that we do perform the service of the LORD in his presence with our burnt offerings and sacrifices and peace offerings, so your children will not say to our children in time to come, "You have no portion in the LORD."

(Joshua 22.26-27, ESV)

And all that generation also were gathered to their fathers. And there arose another generation after them who did not know the LORD or the work that he had done for Israel.

(Judges 2.10, ESV)

And the boy [Samuel] ministered to the LORD in the presence of Eli the priest.

(1 Samuel 2.11, ESV)

So they and their sons were in charge of the gates of the house of the LORD, that is, the house of the tent, as guards.

(1 Chronicles 9.23, ESV)

Meanwhile all Judah stood before the LORD, with their little ones, their wives, and their children.

(2 Chronicles 20.13, ESV)

And they offered great sacrifices that day and rejoiced, for God had made them rejoice with great joy; the women and children also rejoiced. And the joy of Jerusalem was heard far away.

(Nehemiah 12.43, ESV)

All the ends of the earth shall remember
and return to the LORD,
and all the families of the nations
shall worship before you.
For kingship belongs to the LORD,
 and he rules over the nations.
All the prosperous of the earth eat and worship;
before him shall bow all who go down to the dust,
even the one who could not keep himself alive.
Posterity shall serve him;
it shall be told of the Lord to the coming generation;
they shall come and proclaim his righteousness to a people yet unborn,
that he has done it.

(Psalm 22.27-34, ESV)

Walk about Zion, go around her,
number her towers,
consider well her ramparts,
go through her citadels,
that you may tell the next generation
that this is God,
our God forever and ever.
He will guide us forever.

(Psalm 48.12-14, ESV)

So even to old age and gray hairs,
O God, do not forsake me,
until I proclaim your might to another generation,
your power to all those to come.

(Psalm 71.18, ESV)

Give ear, O my people, to my teaching;
incline your ears to the words of my mouth!
I will open my mouth in a parable;
I will utter dark sayings from of old,
things that we have heard and known,
that our fathers have told us.
We will not hide them from their children,
but tell to the coming generation
the glorious deeds of the Lord, and his might,
and the wonders that he has done.
He established a testimony in Jacob
and appointed a law in Israel,
which he commanded our fathers
to teach to their children,
that the next generation might know them,
the children yet unborn,
and arise and tell them to their children,
so that they should set their hope in God
and not forget the works of God,
but keep his commandments,
and that they should not be like their fathers,
a stubborn and rebellious generation,
a generation whose heart was not steadfast,
whose spirit was not faithful to God.

(Psalm 78.1-8, ESV)

But we your people, the sheep of your pasture,
will give thanks to you forever;
from generation to generation we will recount your praise.

85

(Psalm 79.13, ESV)

I will sing of the steadfast love of the LORD, forever;
with my mouth I will make known your faithfulness to all generations.

(Psalm 89.1, ESV)

Let this be recorded for a generation to come,
so that a people yet to be created may praise the LORD.

(Psalm 102.18, ESV)

One generation shall commend your works to another,
and shall declare your mighty acts.

(Psalm 145.4, ESV)

Hear, my son, your father's instruction,
and forsake not your mother's teaching.

(Proverbs 1.8, ESV)

Train up a child in the way he should go;
even when he is old he will not depart from it.

(Proverbs 22.6, ESV)

"Before I formed you in the womb I knew you,
and before you were born I consecrated you;
I appointed you a prophet to the nations."
Then I said, "Ah, Lord God! Behold I do not know how to speak, for I
am only a youth." But the LORD said to me,
"Do not say, 'I am only a youth';
for to all to whom I send you, you shall go,
and whatever I command you, you shall speak.
Do not be afraid of them, for I am with you to deliver you,
declares the LORD."

(Jeremiah 1.5-8, ESV)

Tell your children of it, and let your children tell their children,
and their children to another generation.

(Joel 1.3, ESV)

Blow the trumpet in Zion;
consecrate a fast;
call a solemn assembly;
gather the people.
Consecrate the congregation;
assemble the elders;
gather the children,
even nursing infants.
Let the bridegroom leave his room,
and the bride her chamber.

(Joel 2.15-16, ESV)

New Testament

At that time the disciples came to Jesus, saying, "Who is the greatest in the kingdom of heaven?" And calling to him a child, he put him in the midst of them and said, "Truly, I say to you, unless you turn and become like children, you will never enter the kingdom of heaven. Whoever humbles himself like this child is the greatest in the kingdom of heaven. Whoever receives one such child in my name receives me, but whoever causes one of these little one who believe in me to sin, it would be better for him to have a great millstone fastened around his neck and to be drowned in the depth of the sea."

(Matthew 18.1-6, ESV)

Then children were brought to him that he might lay his hands on them and pray. The disciples rebuked the people, but Jesus said, "Let the little children come to me and do not hinder them, for to such belongs the kingdom of heaven." And he laid his hands on them and went away.

(Matthew 19.13-15, ESV)

And he sat down and called the twelve. And he said to them, "If anyone would be first, he must be last of all and servant of all." And he took a child and put him in the midst of them, and taking him in his arms, he said to them, "Whoever receives one such child in my name receives me, and whoever receives me, receives not me but him who sent me."

(Mark 9.35-37, ESV)

And they were bringing children to him that he might touch them, and the disciples rebuked them. But when Jesus saw it, he was indignant and said to them, "Let the children come to me; do not hinder them, for to such belongs the kingdom of God. Truly, I say to you, whoever does not receive the kingdom of God like a child shall not enter it." And he took them in his arms and blessed them, laying his hands on them.

(Mark 10.13-16, ESV)

An argument arose among them as to which of them was the greatest. But Jesus, knowing the reasoning of their hearts, took a child and put him by his side and said to them, "Whoever receives this child in my name receives me, and whoever receives me receives him who sent me. For he who is least among you all is the one who is great."

(Luke 9.46-48, ESV)

Now they were bringing even infants to him that he might touch them. And when the disciples saw it, they rebuked them. But Jesus called them to him, saying, "Let the children come to me, and do not hinder them, for to such belongs the kingdom of God. Truly, I say to you, whoever does not receive the kingdom of God like a child shall not enter it."

(Luke 18.15-17, ESV)

On the first day of the week, when we were gathered together to break bread, Paul talked with them, intending to depart on the next day, and he prolonged his speech until midnight. There were many lamps in the upper room where we were gathered. And a young man named Eutychus, sitting at the window, sank into a deep sleep as Paul talked still longer. And being overcome by sleep, he fell down from the third story and was taken up dead. But Paul went down and bent over him, and taking him in his arms, said, "Do not be alarmed, for his life is in him." And when Paul had gone up and had broken break and eaten, he conversed with them a long while, until daybreak, and so departed. And they took the youth away alive, and were not a little comforted.

(Acts 20.7-12, ESV)

When our days there were ended, we departed and went on our journey, and they all, with wives and children, accompanied us until we were outside the city. And kneeling down on the beach, we prayed and said farewell to one another. Then we went on board the ship, and they returned home.

(Acts 21.5-6, ESV)

For as in one body we have many members, and the members do not all have the same function, so we, though many, are one body in Christ, and individually members one of another.

(Romans 12.4-5, ESV)

For just as the body is one and has many members, and all the members of the body, though many, are one body, so it is with Christ. For in one Spirit we were all baptized into one body—Jews or Greeks, slaves or free—and all were made to drink of one Spirit.

For the body does not consist of one member but of many. If the foot should say, "Because I am not a hand, I do not belong to the body," that would not make it any less a part of the body. And if the ear should say,

"Because I am not an eye, I do not belong to the body," that would not make it any less a part of the body. If the whole body were an eye, where would be the sense of hearing? If the whole body were an ear, where would be the sense of smell? But as it is, God arranged the members in the body, each one of them, as he chose. If all were a single member, where would the body be? As it is, there are many parts, yet one body.

The eye cannot say to the hand, "I have no need of you," nor again the head to the feet, "I have no need of you." On the contrary, the parts of the body that seem to be weaker are indispensable, and on those parts of the body that we think less honorable we bestow the greater honor, and our unpresentable parts are treated with greater modesty, which our more presentable parts do not require. But God has so composed the body, giving greater honor to the part that lacked it, that there may be no division in the body, but that the members may have the same care for one another. If one member suffers, all suffer together; if one member is honored, all rejoice together.

Now you are the body of Christ and individually members of it.

(1 Corinthians 12.12-27, ESV)

Fathers, do not provoke your children to anger, but bring them up in the discipline and instruction of the Lord.

(Ephesians 6.4, ESV)

Let no one despise you for your youth, but set the believers an example in speech, in conduct, in love, in faith, in purity.

(1 Timothy 4.12, ESV)

Do not rebuke an older man but encourage him as you would a father. Treat younger men like brothers, older women like mothers, younger women like sisters, in all purity.

(1 Timothy 5.1-2, ESV)

Older men are to be sober-minded, dignified, self-controlled, sound in faith, in love, and in steadfastness. Older women likewise are to be reverent in behavior, not slanderers or slaves to much wine. They are to teach what is good, and so train the young women to love their husbands and children.

(Titus 2.2-4, ESV)

Intergenerational Biblical Relationships

Scripture also relates many examples of intergenerational relationships or significant interaction between persons of different generations. Here is a listing of some of those interactions:[86]

- **Moses and Jethro** *(Exodus 18)*
- **Samuel and Eli** *(1 Samuel 2-3)*
- **David and Saul** *(1 Samuel 16-31)*[87]
- **Elijah and Elisha** *(1 Kings 19.19-21; 2 Kings 2; 3.11)*
- **Ruth and Naomi** *(Ruth 1-4)*
- **Mary and Elizabeth** *(Luke 1.39-56)*
- **Simeon and Anna responding to the presentation of the newborn Jesus in the temple** *(Luke 2.22-38)*
- **Twelve-year-old Jesus with the teachers in the temple** *(Luke 2.41-52)*
- **Jesus' disciples and the boy with five loaves and two fish** *(John 6.1-14)*

---

[86] This list comes largely from Allan G. Harkness, "Intergenerationality: Biblical And Theological Foundations," *Christian Education Journal*, 3rd ser., 9 (Spring 2012): 122.

[87] Granted, David and Saul's relationship did not turn out well in the end. Nevertheless, that doesn't change the fact that initially David and Saul had a strong relationship that benefited both parties.

- **Various interactions between Jesus and young people He healed** *(the widow of Nain's son, Luke 7.11-17; Jairus's daughter, Matthew 9.18-19, 23-26, Mark 5.21-24, 35-43, Luke 8.40-42, 49-56, the boy with an evil spirit, Matthew 17.14-21, Mark 9.14-29, Luke 9.37-45)*

- **Barnabas and John Mark** *(Acts 12.25; 13.5; 15.36-39; Colossians 4.10)*

- **Paul and Timothy** *(Acts 16.1-3; 17.14-15; 19.21-22; 20.3-5; Romans 16.21; 1 Corinthians 4.17; 16.10; 2 Corinthians 1.1,19; Philippians 1.1; 2.19; Colossians 1.1; 1 Thessalonians 1.1; 3.1-8; 2 Thessalonians 1.1; 1 Timothy 1.2, 18-19; 4.12; 5.1-2; 6.20-21; 2 Timothy 1.1-6; 2.1-7; 4.9-22; Philemon 1.1)*

- **Paul and Eutychus** *(Acts 20.7-12)*

Appendix B

resources and bibliography

Major Influences

My thoughts in this handbook have been substantially built upon the work and research of others, and thus, I thought it might be beneficial to point you in the direction of some of those resources. The following books have been major influences for me, and would be excellent resources if you are interested in further study on the topics presented here:

Almost Christian: What the Faith of Our Teenagers is Telling the American Church, **by Kenda Creasy Dean (Oxford University Press, 2010).** Dean's book draws heavily on the research of Christian Smith and the National Study of Youth and Religion (NSYR). Among other things, she makes the important observations that most American Christian teenagers are unable to put their faith into words, and also that "Christianity" as practiced by the average Christian teenager is very different from what Christianity has historically meant and taught for the last 2,000 years.

Family-Based Youth Ministry: Revised and Expanded, **by Mark DeVries (IVP Books, 2004).** This is an updated version of DeVries's original book, and in many ways, he is a pioneer in the field of family ministry. DeVries presents a lot of excellent food for thought for youth ministers, including the dangers of age segregation, the great amount of influence that parents have on their children, and the importance of youth ministers sticking around with the same congregation long enough to make a difference.

Hurt 2.0: Inside the World of Today's Teenagers, **by Chap Clark (Baker Academic, 2011).** This is probably the most depressing of all the books described here because it is largely filled with bad news, namely, that teens live in a world that is characterized by risky behaviors and is poorly understood by parents and other adults. Nevertheless, it is an important book, because it discusses in detail the problem of age segregation in our society and the way it inhibits healthy growth and development in adolescents.

Intergenerational Christian Formation: Bringing the Whole Church Together in Ministry, Community and Worship, **by Holly Catterton Allen and Christine Lawton Ross (IVP Academic, 2012).** The title explains exactly what this book is about. While other books such as *Family-Based Youth Ministry, Soul Searching,* and *Sticky Faith* discuss the importance of intergenerationality, this book is the most comprehensive examination of that topic I have found.

Soul Searching: The Religious and Spiritual Lives of American Teenagers, **by Christian Smith with Melinda Lundquist Denton,(Oxford University Press, 2005).** This is a very important book in which sociologist Christian Smith examines the data from the NSYR and draws significant conclusions from it. Most tellingly, he argues that the predominant religion practiced by most American teenagers is something called "Moralistic Therapeutic Deism", a faith system that is largely built on being nice, and is nothing more than a "misbegotten step-cousin" of Christianity. Smith's book is harder to read than the rest in this list, but is an excellent resource, and provides much of the analysis upon which *Almost Christian* is based.

Sticky Faith: Everyday Ideas to Build Lasting Faith in Your Kids, **by Kara E. Powell and Chap Clark (Zondervan, 2011).** If I had to pick one single book outside of the Bible which really revolutionized the way I view youth ministry, this would be it. Drawing on extensive research and interviews with teenagers, *Sticky Faith* is especially geared towards parents, and is filled with practical ideas for ways in which parents (and to a lesser degree, churches) can encourage lifelong faith in their children.

The Lunch Ladies: Cultivating an Actsmosphere, **by Philip Jenkins (2015).** Basically, *Lunch Ladies* details the story of how the youth ministry which Jenkins leads was changed from a culture of indifference and neglect to one where Christ's love was shown to every person who came through the doors. It is a powerful and inspiring story, and has had a significant impact on our youth ministry (it is easy and fun to read as well!).

The Sticky Faith Guide For Your Family, **by Kara E. Powell (Zondervan, 2014).** The content of this book is very similar to *Sticky Faith,* but the focus of *The Sticky Faith Guide* is different, as it spends less time on presenting research and instead heavily emphasizes the practical, with over 100 specific ideas of activities that families can try to build lasting faith in their kids. This is an excellent and accessible resource for families.

Why They Left: Listening to Those Who Have Left Churches of Christ, **by Flavil R. Yeakley, Jr. (Gospel Advocate, 2012).** This is not a book about youth ministry, but it does touch on the issue of young people in Churches of Christ leaving the church after high school, and also emphasizes that the more legitimate relationships a person develops within a congregation, the more likely they are to stay. This obviously has implications for youth ministry.

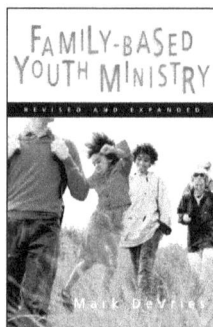

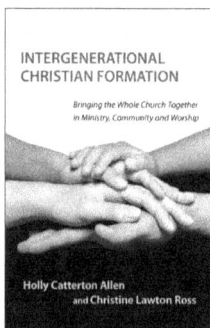

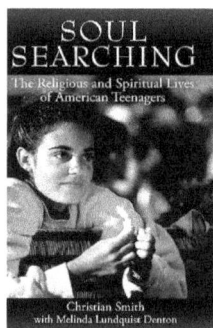

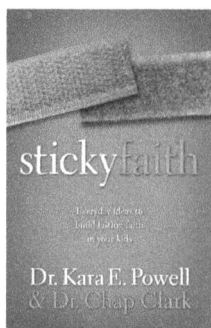

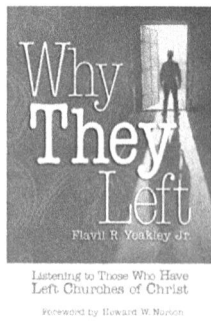

Bibliography

Allen, Holly Catterton. "Guest Editorial: Bringing The Generations Back Together: Introduction To Intergenerationality." *Christian Education Journal*, 3rd ser., 9 (Spring 2012): 101-4.

Allen, Holly Catterton and Christine Lawton Ross. *Intergenerational Christian Formation: Bringing the Whole Church Together in Ministry, Community and Worship.* Downers Grove, IL: IVP Academic, 2012.

Bell, Rob. *Velvet Elvis: Repainting the Christian Faith.* Grand Rapids, MI: Zondervan, 2005.

Black, Wesley. "Youth Ministry That Lasts: The Faith Journey Of Young Adults." *Journal of Youth Ministry* 4, no. 2 (Spring 2006): 19-48.

Briggs, David. "The No. 1 Reason Teens Keep the Faith as Young Adults." *Huffington Post* (October 29, 2014), http://www.huffingtonpost.com/david-briggs/the-no-1-reason-teens-kee_b_6067838.html (accessed January 15, 2016).

Clark, Chap. *Hurt 2.0: Inside the World of Today's Teenagers.* Grand Rapids, MI: Baker Academic, 2011.

Csikszentmihalyi, Mihaly and Carson Reed. *Being Adolescent: Conflict and Growth in the Teenage Years.* New York: Basic Books, 1984.

Dean, Kenda Creasy. *Almost Christian: What the Faith of Our Teenagers Is Telling the American Church.* Oxford: Oxford University Press, 2010.

_____. "Proclaiming Salvation: Youth Ministry for the Twenty-First Century Church." *Theology Today* 56, no. 4 (January 2000): 524-39.

DeVries, Mark. *Family-Based Youth Ministry.* Rev. ed. Downers Grove, IL: InterVarsity Press, 2004.

Dill, Ellen Renee. "Planning for All Ages: Intergenerational Events Can Build Bridges in a Church." *The Christian Ministry* 17, no. 2 (March 1986): 16-18.

Dixon, Stephen W. "What's So Special About Children? A Reconsideration of the Use Made of Scriptures such as Matthew 18:1-5 in Advocating the Importance of Children for the Church." *Journal of Childhood and Religion* 5, no. 1 (January 2014): 1-33.

Duerksen, Carol. *Building Together: Developing Your Blueprint for Congregational Youth Ministry.* Newton, KS: Faith & Life Resources, 2001.

Fishbane, Mona DeKoven. "'Honor Thy Father and Thy Mother': Intergenerational Spirituality and Jewish Tradition." In *Spiritual Resources in Family Therapy,* edited by Froma Walsh, 136-56. New York: Guilford Press, 1999.

Furnish, Dorothy Jean. "Rethinking Children's Ministry." In *Rethinking Christian Education: Explorations in Theory and Practice,* edited by David S. Schuller, 73-84. St. Louis: Chalice Press, 1993.

Glassford, Darwin and Lynn Barger-Elliot. "Toward Intergenerational Ministry in a Post-Christian Era." *Christian Education Journal* 8, no. 2 (September 2011): 364-78.

Harkness, Allan G. "Intergenerational and Homogenous-Age Education: Mutually Exclusive Strategies for Faith Communities?" *Religious Education* 95, no. 1 (Winter 2000): 51-63.

_____. "Intergenerational Christian Education: An Imperative for Effective Education in Local Churches, Part 1." *Journal of Christian Education* 41, no. 2 (July 1998): 5-14.

_____. "Intergenerational Corporate Worship as a Significant Educational Activity." *Christian Education Journal* 7, no. 1 (2003): 5-21.

_____. "Intergenerational Education for an Intergenerational Church?" *Religious Education* 93, no. 4 (Fall 1998): 431-47.

_____. "Intergenerationality: Biblical And Theological Foundations." *Christian Education Journal,* 3rd ser., 9 (Spring 2012): 121-34.

Hawkins, Faith Kirkham. "Ministry With Youth...Without Youth Ministry." *Insights* 123, no. 2 (Spring 2008): 26-30.

Hinrichs, Harold J. "Intergenerational Living and Worship: The Caring Community." *Journal of Religion and Aging* 3, nos. 1-2 (September 1986): 181-92.

Joiner, Reggie. *Think Orange: Imagine the Impact When Church And Family Collide.* Colorado Springs: David C. Cook, 2009.

Joiner, Reggie and Tom Shefchunas. *Lead Small: Five Big Ideas Every Small Group Leader Needs To Know.* Cumming, GA: reThink Group, 2012.

Jones, Timothy Paul. *Family Ministry Field Guide: How Your Church Can Equip Parents to Make Disciples.* Indianapolis: Wesleyan Publishing House, 2011.

Martinson, Roland D. *Effective Youth Ministry: A Congregational Approach.* Minneapolis: Augsburg Publishing House, 1988.

A Matter of Time: Risk and Opportunity in the Nonschool Hours. Report of the Task Force on Youth Development and Community Programs. Washington, DC: Carnegie Council on Adolescent Development, 1992.

Meehan, Bridget M. "Family-Centered Intergenerational Religious Education: Families Minister to Families." *Military Chaplains' Review* (1989): 39-45.

Nelson, Bryan and Timothy Paul Jones. "The Problem and the Promise of Family Ministry." *Journal of Family Ministry* 1 (Fall-Winter 2010): 36-43.

Nelson, C. Ellis. "Spiritual Formation: A Family Matter." *Journal of Family Ministry* 20 (Fall 2006): 13-27.

O'Keefe, Theresa. "Growing Up Alone: The New Normal of Isolation in Adolescence." *The Journal of Youth Ministry* 13, no. 1 (September 2014): 63-84.

Powell, Kara E. *The Sticky Faith Guide For Your Family.* Grand Rapids, MI: Zondervan, 2014.

Powell, Kara E., and Chap Clark. *Sticky Faith: Everyday Ideas to Build Lasting Faith in Your Kids.* Grand Rapids, MI: Zondervan, 2011.

Plummer, Robert L. "Bring Them Up in the Discipline and Instruction of the Lord." *Journal of Family Ministry* 1 (Fall-Winter 2010): 18-26.

Richter, Don C., Doug Magnuson, and Michael Baizerman. "Reconceiving Youth Ministry." *Religious Education* 93, no. 3 (Summer 1998): 340-57.

Roehlkepartain, Jolene L. "Innovative Ways to Build an Effective Family Ministry." *Journal of Family Ministry* 15 (Winter 2001): 12-20.

Ross, Christine M. "Four Congregations That Practice Intergenerationality." *Christian Education Journal*, 3rd ser., 9 (Spring 2012): 135-47.

Rost, Robert A. "Intergenerational Relationships Within the Local Congregation." *Journal of Religious Gerontology* 13, no. 2 (2001): 55-68.

Smith, Christian with Melinda Lundquist Denton. *Soul Searching: The Religious and Spiritual Lives of American Teenagers.* Oxford: Oxford University Press, 2005.

Smith, Christian with Patricia Snell. *Souls in Transition: The Religious and Spiritual Lives of Emerging Adults.* Oxford: Oxford University Press, 2009.

Snailum, Brenda. "Implementing Intergenerational Youth Ministry Within Existing Congregations: What Have We Learned?" *Christian Education Journal*, 3rd ser., 9 (Spring 2012): 165-81.

_____. "Integrating Intergenerational Ministry Strategies into Existing Youth Ministries: What can a Hybrid Approach be Expected to Accomplish?" *The Journal of Youth Ministry* 11, no. 2 (2013): 7-28.

Tidwell, J. "The Child in the Church." *Journal of Christian Education Papers* 64 (1979): 23. Quoted in Allan G. Harkness, "Intergenerational Corporate Worship as a Significant Educational Activity." *Christian Education Journal* 7, no. 1 (2003): 5-21.

Win, Stuart. "How Far Is Too Far? Segregation versus Integration in Youth Ministry." *St. Mark's Review* 225, no. 3 (2013): 128-37.

Witherington, Ben III. *Conflict & Community in Corinth: A Socio-Rhetorical Commentary on 1 & 2 Corinthians.* Grand Rapids: Eerdmans, 1995.

Yeakley, Jr., Flavil R. *Why They Left: Listening to Those Who Have Left Churches of Christ.* Nashville: Gospel Advocate, 2012.

Image Credits

*Unless otherwise noted below, images for this book were either uncredited, belong to the author, or came from **www.unsplash.com,** a wonderful, totally free source for high-resolution photographs.*

Page 9: David Lindner, https://www.flickr.com/photos/lindnerphotographic/6626537367/

Page 11: Basket USA, http://www.basketusa.com/medias/internet/18431/dossiers-de-lete-comment-trouver-un-playground-pres-de-chez-soi/

Page 20: Infographic courtesy of Deeper Youth Ministry.

Page 24: "White's Bog: 1910", available on shorpy.com at http://www.shorpy.com/node/5661

Page 32: "Photos of country churches", http://www.toddklassy.com/montana-blog/2015/9/22/photos-of-country-churches

Page 37: Matt Neale, "The carved busts of Socrates, Antisthenes, Chrysippus, and Epicurus", https://en.wikipedia.org/wiki/Philosophy_of_happiness#/media/File:Greek_philosopher_busts.jpg

Page 55: Image courtesy of Farmington Church of Christ.

Page 75: Life of Jesus Christ, http://www.jesus-story.net/painting_jesus_children.htm

Page 79: American Bible Society, http://news.americanbible.org/blog/entry/bible-blog/10-ways-to-teach-the-bible-to-children

ABOUT THE AUTHOR

Luke Dockery serves as the Associate Minister of the Farmington Church of Christ, where he has been since 2006. He loves teenagers, and is devoted to helping them develop a mature and lasting faith in Jesus Christ.

Luke and his wife Caroline have two children, Kinsley and Seth. Luke is a graduate of Harding University, and received his Master of Divinity degree from Harding School of Theology in 2018.

In his free time, Luke enjoys spending time with his family, reading, playing ultimate frisbee, and cheering for the Arkansas Razorbacks and Atlanta Braves.

TWITTER: @thedocfile | FACEBOOK: www.facebook.com/lukedockery
WEB: www.lukedockery.com | INSTAGRAM: instagram.com/thedocfile

www.ingramcontent.com/pod-product-compliance
Lightning Source LLC
Chambersburg PA
CBHW062007040426
42447CB00010B/1949